Where
Wilderness
Preservation
Began

Where Wilderness Preservation Began

Adirondack Writings of Howard Zahniser

Edited with an Introduction by
Ed Zahniser

And Commentary by
George D. Davis
Paul Schaefer
Douglas W. Scott

Published by
North Country Books, Inc.
18 Irving Place
Utica, New York

Where Wilderness Preservation Began:
Adirondack Writings of Howard Zahniser

ISBN 0-932052-76-2

Library of Congress Cataloging-in-Publication Data

Zahniser, Howard.
    Where wilderness preservation began: Adirondack writings of
Howard Zahniser / edited with an introduction by Ed Zahniser
and commentary by George D. Scott, Paul Schaefer, Douglas W.
Scott.
        p. cm.
    ISBN 0-932052-76-2
    1. Zahniser, Howard—Diaries. 2. Nature conservation—New
York (State)—Adirondack Mountains. 3. Adirondack Forest
Preserve (N.Y.). 4. Wilderness areas—New York (State). 5.
Conservationists—United States—Biography.   I. Zahniser,
Ed.   II. Scott, George D.   III. Schaefer, Paul.   IV. Scott,
Douglas W. V. Title.
QH31.Z34A3   1992
33.78'216'097475—dc20   92-26040
                                                              CIP

Published by
North Country Books, Inc.
Publisher—Distributor
18 Irving Place
Utica, New York 13501

*This book is dedicated to
Alice B. Zahniser
Esther Zahniser
Karen Zahniser Bettacchi
and the coming generations*

CONTENTS

The Wilderness Society's Governing Council meeting in 1946 included, front row left, Harvey Broome, Aldo Leopold, Irving M. Clark, Mrs. Laurette Collier, Ernest C. Oberholtzer, Robert Griggs, and Bernard Frank, and, back row, Benton MacKay, Olaus Murie, George Marshall, Howard Zahniser, Harold Anderson, Charles Woodbury, and Ernest Griffith. George Marshall is a brother of Robert Marshall, the Society's founding force and endower, who had died in 1938 at age 39.

Introduction

Howard Zahniser accepted the position as executive secretary of The Wilderness Society in 1945. His wife Alice Hayden Zahniser was then pregnant with their fourth child. The new job meant leaving a successful and promising civil service career at half the salary. Despite the impressive job title, Zahnie, as friends and associates called him, was the Society's only full-time paid staff person. Pragmatically, the job move was ill-advised. Zahnie, however, was a pragmatist only as a last resort. Fundamentally he was an optimist. He had to be: in the mid-1940s there was no broad-based environmental movement, and few people had even heard of conservation.

Zahnie inherited his optimism. His father, pastor of a struggling church, made 227 pastoral calls during the first quarter of the year of his death. Zahnie's zealous wilderness advocacy reflected his faith that anyone could be persuaded that wilderness was essential to the "eternity of the future." Without wilderness, he maintained, humanity would find itself both materially and spiritually impoverished. In 1964, the year of his fatal heart attack just four months before the Wilderness Act became law, Zahnie also made his quota of pastoral calls—on Capitol Hill, in executive offices, at newspapers, and in the offices of his conservationist peers—lobbying and promoting its prospects and keeping his coalition together.

Paul A. Schaefer introduced Zahnie to the wilderness of the Adirondacks, recruiting him and The Wilderness Society to the defense of its "forever wild" Forest Preserve lands. Schaefer invited Zahnie and family to his cabin for a 1946 summer vacation. With but few exceptions for forays into western wilderness areas, the family would continue to vacation in the Adirondacks—and does so today. This book collects Zahnie's heretofore unpublished journal of that 1946 trip with important testimony delivered in Albany in 1953, and his speech to the New York State Conservation Council in 1957 on behalf

1

of Adirondack wilderness. (The 1957 speech has been edited for some duplication of material in the 1953 testimony.) The book also includes his essay, "The Need for Wilderness," first delivered as a speech in 1955, a year before the first Wilderness Bill was introduced in Congress.

Zahnie's Adirondack wilderness writings are significant for two reasons. First, their summary of America's cultural valuation of wilderness contains an early formulation of the national need for protecting it by legislative means such as provided in New York State. Second, Zahnie cites this constitutional protection as a model for securing a similar level of protection for federal wilderness resources. These mark important steps, in 1946 and 1953, toward the soon-to-be-launched, protracted struggle that would culminate in the Wilderness Act of 1964 and its establishment of the National Wilderness Preservation System. That Wilderness System's fate lies now in the hands of the U.S. Congress. Designated wilderness is no longer subject to the administrative whims of federal land management agencies.

Taken together, these writings afford personal and professional insights into what Doug Scott calls "The Visionary Role of Howard Zahniser," the architect of wilderness. The man who left federal service to work for an obscure conservation organization matured with that organization as a national force for the environment. It is fitting that a founder of and driving force behind The Wilderness Society had been Robert Marshall, whose wilderness advocacy was steeped in his Adirondack heritage. That the nation owes a debt to the Adirondacks and New York State for these men's advocacy for wilderness preservation is made clear in "Wilderness: New York Sets a Global Stage" by George Davis, who served as executive director of The Governor's Commission on the Adirondacks in the 21st Century. Zahnie's writings acknowledge his debt, and the nation's, to the Adirondack experience. In 1989, for the 25th anniversary of the Wilderness Act, the Adirondack Council placed a plaque on the Mateskared cabin recognizing the intimate connection between Zahnie's Adirondack experiences and the Wilderness Act. David Gibson, executive director of the Association for the Protection of the Adirondacks writes that "plans were set in motion by the Adirondack

Council, supported by the Association for the Protection of the Adirondacks and the Adirondack Mountain Club, to honor the Wilderness Act's author, Howard Zahniser. There was absolutely no doubt where this commemoration would take place." Governor Mario Cuomo had issued a proclamation declaring the week of September 3 to September 9 as Wilderness Week, and his representatives were planning to attend a special ceremony at the Zahniser cabin in Bakers Mills.

"Thanks to organizational work by the Adirondack Council," Gibson writes, "September 6 brought seasonable weather and dozens of conservationists to the top of Edwards Hill Road. There they greeted Alice Zahniser, and many of her friends and neighbors in Bakers Mills who had known Howard during his many sojourns to this special place, where wilderness preservation truly began. Paul Schaefer led half a dozen leaders of Adirondack organizations up from his cabin, situated just 100 yards downhill. . . There were gathered the governor's representatives, Woody Cole, chairman of the Adirondack Park agency, and Robert Binnewies, deputy commissioner for natural resources for the Department of Environmental Conservation."

In all, some 100 people crowded together on the rocky knoll beside the cabin. They heard speeches unveiling the Adirondack Council's proposal for a Bob Marshall Great Wilderness in the west-central Adirondack Park. Gibson characterizes the proposal as "a 400,000-acre dream of the late Bob Marshall and made possible by the great legislative national vision of Howard Zahniser." After Paul Schaefer told the group about his first meetings with Marshall and Zahniser, as recounted in the Afterword to this book, the governor's representatives presented the plaque to Alice Zahniser. The Adirondack Council presented her with a hand-carved loon as symbol of wilderness lakes, and the Association for the Protection of the Adirondacks gave her a framed copy of the governor's wilderness proclamation.

Special thanks are due to Paul Schaefer for his many contributions to this book. They go far beyond his illuminating words and photographs herein, for he has been a stalwart defender of the Adirondacks from age 11. He has also been my lifelong Adirondack tutor and inspiration. Doug Scott, conservation director of the Sierra Club, and Jonathan King, editor of its *Sierra* magazine, kindly granted permission to reprint "The Visionary Role of Howard Zahniser." I hope that Doug someday writes the whole story, which he knows so well from his many years of research into—and continuing commitment to carrying forward—the legislative history of the Wilderness Act. Thanks are also due to The Wilderness Society, in whose magazine Paul Schaefer's article originally appeared, under the editorship of Michael Nadel, whose conservation roots are also Adirondack and whose tenacity in defense of wilderness has been exemplary. The Wilderness Society also provided a grant to support producing the book. John Dunlop, editor of New York State's *The Conservationist* magazine, granted permission to reprint the article by George Davis.

Finally, I wish to express appreciation and gratitude to Lee and Helen Zahniser Snyder, without whose lifelong creative encouragement and immediate, practical support for this venture, the book might not have come into being.

P erhaps a personal observation is not amiss. In the 1946 Adirondack journal my father recounts that conservationist John Apperson has named his boat *Article XIV, Section 1*. This is the section of the New York State Constitution that contains the "forever wild" clause protecting Adirondack wilderness. During the intense lobbying effort for the Wilderness Bills in the 1950s, my sister Karen's teddy bear carried a double appellation that reflected our father's similar delight in wordplay. The bear's two nicknames were Wilderness Bill and Gladly the Cross-eyed Bear. The latter is a take-off on the gospel song, "Gladly the Cross I'd Bear."

Delight in words led my father on a long search for the right one to characterize wilderness in its definition in the legislation. He finally chose *untrammeled*. The importance of choosing this qualitative word—since often misquoted as *untrampled*, in fact—became clear in the successful battle to add eastern national forest lands to the Wilderness System in the 1970s. Most of these lands were not pristine but had recovered from human use to the extent that Congress found them now untrammeled. Now New York State, which designated its own State wilderness areas in the 1970s, is not alone among eastern states in having secured within its boundary just such precious resources in perpetuity.

Throughout the years of lobbying for a federal Wilderness Act, Zahnie traveled often to the Adirondacks for rest and renewal. New York State's Constitution provided a precedent for the legislative protection for wilderness that Zahnie envisioned.

Wilderness: New York Sets a Global Stage

George D. Davis

Recognition and respect for wilderness as a distinct resource, a resource in need of protection and management, has existed globally for only a dozen years or so. The first World Wilderness Congress emerged from an idea developed jointly by a Zulu game warden and a white South African—clear evidence that wilderness and respect for nature transcend vast cultural differences. The first congress was held in South Africa in 1977. Others have been held in Australia (1980), Scotland (1983) and the United States (1987). At the fourth World Wilderness Congress over 65 countries were represented by 1,700 participants. As with so many conservation initiatives, the United States was the leader in the wilderness preservation field, having established a National Wilderness Preservation System in 1964.

In New York State the wilderness has been accepted as a legitimate land classification not for a dozen years nor for a quarter century, but for more than a century. New York State first created its renowned Forest Preserve, to be "forever kept as wild forest lands," through legislation enacted in 1885. Constitutional protection was bestowed by the citizens of New York in an 1894 referendum. Specific wilderness designations within the Forest Preserve, where not only the forest would be preserved but no motorized uses of any type would be tolerated, were proposed by a legislative committee in 1960 and officially adopted in 1972. Today's Adirondack Park wilderness system consists of 16 units totaling one million acres while the Catskill Park wilderness system, created by DEC in 1985, includes four units and 100,997 acres.

How did New York's wilderness leadership help shape a national—and subsequently, global—awakening?

The principal founder of The Wilderness Society—the prime force behind the creation of the National Wilderness Preservation System—was a young New Yorker who learned the ways of wilderness in the vast Forest Preserve of the Adirondack's High Peaks and Cranberry Lake regions. Robert (Bob) Marshall, middle son of Louis Marshall, a champion of individual liberties and co-author and defender of the constitutional amendment protecting New York's Forest Preserves, was a human dynamo. Based on his experiences at the family camp on Lower Saranac Lake, at the New York State College of Forestry summer camp on Cranberry Lake and as a member of the first party to have climbed all Adirondack Peaks over 4,000 feet, Marshall embarked on a career that resulted in millions of acres administratively classified as wilderness, wild or primitive in the National Forest System, wilderness resource recognition on Indian lands and numerous articles in professional journals on the value of wilderness. Dead in 1939 at age 38, Bob Marshall's spirit still rides with all Americans who believe in the wilderness cause.

The man who most epitomized Marshall's spirit and coupled that spirit with persistence, dedication and patience was undoubtedly Howard Zahniser, the author of this nation's Wilderness Act. Zahniser, or "Zahnie" as his friends called him, was a Pennsylvanian who derived much of his wilderness knowledge and dedication from the Adirondacks and gave much back to the Adirondacks. And the story of how the Adirondack wilderness had a strong influence on Zahniser and in the shaping of the Wilderness Act is well worth the telling.

Stewart Udall in *The Quiet Crisis and the Next Generation* (1988) had this to say about Howard Zahniser: "In 1946 [seven] years after Marshall's untimely death, Howard Zahniser picked up the torch of Bob's crusade when he left his position in the federal government and became the paid executive of the Wilderness Society's one man operation in Washington. Some surely regarded the bookish, low key Zahniser as a poor choice to spearhead a national campaign for a radical reform. 'Zahnie' was a reserved man, but he had attributes that made him an ideal person to lead the dogged 18-year effort that ensued. He had an uncommon capacity for friendship, he wrote poetry, he adored Thoreau and had an affinity for the Book of Job. These were traits and interests that gave Howard Zahniser the faith and patience he needed to continue his seemingly unending walks in Washington's corridors of power.

"In his first years at the helm of the society, 'Zahnie' acquired vital insights into wilderness values on hikes in the same Adirondack expanses that had earlier fired the imagination of Bob Marshall. Moreover, when he presented testimony to the New York Legislature in support of the 'Forever Wild' covenant in the state's constitution, Zahniser formulated in his mind some of the basic concepts he later incorporated into the initial wilderness bill he submitted to his friends in Congress."

Paul Schaefer is a building contractor from Schenectady who over the course of a lifetime has been a persistent, knowledgeable and devoted advocate of the Adirondacks. During one of Schaefer's presentations pleading for the preservation of the Moose River country of the west central Adirondacks, Howard Zahniser happened to be in the audience. After Schaefer's talk Zahniser approached him, introduced himself, and said on behalf of The Wilderness Society, "We want to help." Never one to miss an opportunity, Paul Schaefer invited him to visit the Adirondacks. The resultant trip in August of 1946, introduced Howard Zahniser to the Adirondacks, an Adirondacks he immediately fell in love with and fought for the remainder of his life.

Schaefer and guide Ed Richard took Zahniser to Adirondack Loj, and from there to Avalanche Pass, Flowed Lands and Hanging Spear Falls on the Opalescent. It was at Hanging Spear Falls that Schaefer described to him his meeting with Bob Marshall on the summit of Mount Marcy 14 years earlier when Marshall told Schaefer "We simply must band together—all of us who love the wilderness. We must fight together—wherever and whenever wilderness is attacked. We must mobilize all our resources, all of our energies, all of our devotion to the wilderness." Zahniser, with his fledgling Wilderness Society, was putting together such an organization. While at Hanging Spear Falls, he told Schaefer of his dream: "In addition to such protection as national parks and monuments now are given, we need some strong legislation which will be similar in effect on a national scale to what Article XIV, Section 1, is to the New York State Forest

10

Preserve. We need to reclaim for the people, perhaps through their representatives in the congress, control over the wilderness regions of America."

Returning from the High Peaks to Schaefer's cabin near Bakers Mills, Zahniser expressed an interest in having a piece of land in the Adirondacks for a cabin site. After dinner while Zahniser and Ed Richard talked, Paul Schaefer decided to hike over to see his friend, hermit "Bobcat" Ranney. Along the way he met a native who was about to move from the hill. He asked Schaefer to let him know if he ever came across anyone who would like to buy his cabin and 21 acres on a nearby mountainside. Paul Schaefer said he thought he might have just the person, and asked what he would take for the property. He named a modest sum and Schaefer immediately gave him a 10 dollar bill—the only money he had with him—as a deposit, received a receipt and returned to his cabin. Here he asked Zahniser and Ed Richard to come with him a half mile through the woods to a point near the edge of what is now the Siamese Ponds Wilderness. Here was the cabin and 21 acres of land. Looking out across the valley at Crane Mountain in the distance, Schaefer asked Zahniser, "Is this something you would like to have?" He replied, "You bet, but I could never afford anything like this." Schaefer smiled, handed him a receipt, and said, "Well, it is yours" and told him to have the rest of the money in 30 days. Which he did.

Thus began an 18-year friendship between the Schaefers and the Zahnisers and a love affair between Zahniser and the Adirondacks. Zahniser's family has spent every summer since 1946 at this cabin, which he named "Mateskared" after his four children, Mathias, Esther, Karen and Edward.

Zahniser not only took preservation ideas and inspiration from the Adirondacks, he also gave to Adirondack preservation. From 1946 until his death in 1964, Zahniser attended innumerable Adirondack meetings and conferences, testified at many hearings on Adirondacks issues, and successfully sought national support of organized labor and national conservation groups for Adirondack issues. He was profoundly impressed with the depth of knowledge and commitment to wilderness frequently expressed by Karl Frederick, Lithgow

Osborne and Herman Forester, leading members of the Association for the Protection of the Adirondacks.

It could be said that Howard Zahniser initiated the eventually successful effort to designate portions of the Adirondack Forest Preserve as wilderness, where natural processes would reign and all motorized equipment would be prohibited. In an eloquent statement presented to the New York State Joint Legislative Committee on Natural Resources in 1953, Zahniser set forth his vision for a wilderness system throughout the United States. Far ahead of his time, he noted that we must do more than merely set areas aside, we must protect them from ourselves. He commented, ". . . We must not only protect the wilderness from commercial exploitation. We must also see that we do not ourselves destroy its wilderness character in our own management programs. We must remember always that the essential quality of the wilderness is its wildness." These words apply equally well today as we continually remind ourselves that wilderness is primarily for the preservation of wildness, not the pleasure of humans.

Zahniser pointed out before the committee the importance of Adirondack wilderness and the trust that the people of New York hold for the rest of the United States. . . . A rising man in the legislature, Assemblyman R. Watson Pomeroy, listened intently to Zahniser's statement on the importance of wilderness. He was profoundly moved. Following the speech, Pomeroy turned to Schaefer and remarked, "There's a man we have to listen to, I believe he has an overview we just don't have." When R. Watson Pomeroy became chairman of the Joint Legislative Committee on Natural Resources in 1959, his first action was to direct committee staff to make a professional inventory of potential Adirondack Forest Preserve wilderness areas.

In the fall of 1957, Howard Zahniser was asked to address the annual convention of the New York State Conservation Council. The council had been active in supporting Adirondack preservation matters for a number of years, but it was Zahniser's address that rallied them to the specific cause of wilderness preservation within the Adirondack and Catskill Forest Preserves.

Zahniser titled his address "Where Wilderness Preservation Began" for he sincerely felt that it was in New York State's Adirondacks and Catskills that, in a very real sense, the national wilderness preservation movement began. Zahniser outlined the history of the Forest Preserve, and described how much more the "forever wild" concept is than mere recreation. He stated that the central purpose of the wilderness bill, which he had drafted for Senator Hubert Humphrey and Representative John Saylor the previous year, was "To spread from here throughout the nation the kind of program you (in New York State) have worked out here through the years.

During this entire period, Zahniser was in failing health, and the long hours, the many hearings he attended at which he frequently gave testimony, and the general anxiety over the eventual outcome of what had become the work of his life had left him weak and exhausted.

Writing to Paul Schaefer on April 29, 1964, Zahniser noted that "The 19th hearings on the wilderness legislation are underway this week, and the prospect of *something* seems better than ever. I testified again yesterday and survived the questioning, but was soaked and breathless. The prospect for a post-wilderness-bill-controversy period of book writing doesn't seem too good. My best boast now is that I am better than I ever will be." And then he added, somewhat wistfully, "When will the lilacs bloom on the hillside above 'Mateskared?' Wouldn't we enjoy seeing them and smelling them?"

On May 4, 1964, six days after giving testimony on the bill he had originally drafted eight years earlier, Howard Zahniser died. Despite the 66 rewritings of the wilderness bill that followed his first draft, the final Wilderness Act was still Howard Zahniser's, epitomized by the definitional phrase he had sought for months: "untrammeled by man." His end was really the beginning as President Johnson recognized in signing the Wilderness Act four months later.

The nine million acres that became wilderness upon that signature, as the beginning of the National Wilderness Preservation System, have now, 25 years later, grown to 90 million acres. The concept has been picked up by dozens of nations abroad from Australia to the

Soviet Union. Zahniser's dream is becoming a global reality. And it all began right here in New York State.

George D. Davis is the principal partner in Davis Associates land use policy consulting firm. He has also served as executive director of The Wilderness Society and executive director of Governor Cuomo's Commission on the Adirondacks in the Twenty-First Century. He is a recipient of the prestigious John D. and Catherine T. MacArthur Foundation Award.

Karen, Esther, and Mathias (from front to back) near the base of Eleventh Mountain on the edge of today's Siamese Ponds Wilderness, possibly on the trip to Mud Pond and Second Pond Flow on Monday, July 29.

To the Adirondacks July-August 1946

Howard Zahniser

Friday, July 26.—After much rushing—Alice in packing and preparing, I in getting writings and other work done and in shape— we left Hyattsville [Maryland] with Mathias, Esther, and Karen about 7 a.m., going first to the Spencerville campground to take a screen that Alice's mother needed at her cottage. I visited with a few, leaving some Wilderness Society folders, and greeted Bishop Pearce. Mother [Annie Esther Peverill] Hayden, Aunt Ella, Faith, and Joyce saw us off from there. We ate a lunch Alice had packed, at Gettsyburg [Pennsylvania], the children and I climbing a tower while it was being spread. The trip up the Susquehanna was lovely, but so was the whole day, especially the last part across the hills to Vestal, N.Y., where we arrived about 6.30 and had a delicious roast beef dinner with Sis and Guy—after which Guy took all of us to Endicott and to Binghamton, showing us points of interest—particularly the International Business Machine plant where he is employed and the luxurious and comfortable club house maintained for I.B.M. employees. Back at Williams's, we saw slides of Watkins Glen and Guy and I visited till after midnight. It had been a great first day—and the weather as lovely as a day can be.

Sat. July 27.—After a good breakfast and some picture taking, we left Vestal about 10 a.m. (time from here on is Daylight Savings). We passed through Binghamton expeditiously with the aid of a map and directions from Guy—and continued on N.Y. Route 7 to Schenectady. Once again the weather gave the day the best of loveliness. The Susquehanna was interesting; and the hills were inviting, the Adirondacks that we saw now and then as we came near Schenectady having a real welcome and blue nobility. One event was exciting. A team of work horses ran from a barn toward the road (a disobedient boy, as it turned out, riding one). I slowed down to give them a chance to cross ahead. Then unexpectedly they wheeled and re-crossed the road in front of me. My brakes skidded the tires, but I struck the near horse lightly (at about 5 miles per hour by then) and we saw the team continue on to the barn. At a place where we stopped for gasoline the children enjoyed a romp, see-sawing, and swinging. We arrived at Paul Schaefer's [at 897 St. Davids Lane, Schenectady] on time as expected, there met Carolyn (Paul's wife) and the children Mary, 10; Evelyn, 6; Francis, 3; and Monica, 3 months. Also Carolyn's brother Nathaniel Keseberg and "Red." We did some re-packing and started out from there with two cars, Mary with us, our top down for the first time on the trip. At Northville we ate, and then continued to Bakers Mills (Alice driving with Mary, Mathias, and Karen up front and Esther and I trying to keep warm in a delicious coldness in the back, Esther all wrapped in a car blanket, boxes filling up the air space beside us.) We arrived at Schaefer's cottages 1.8 miles up from Bakers Mills, under a spur of Eleventh Mountain, looking out to the East on a magnificent distant view of Crane Mountain, just before dark, in time only to unload and make some beds and retire happy.

Sunday, July 28.—Instead of "getting settled" I drove Carolyn and her children (saving the baby, with Alice) to mass at Wevertown. When we returned Paul Schaefer had arrived, and we visited with him, doing nothing as to the trip except discussing equipment, but rather going over in detail the problems and philosophy of the wilderness. He is a real person. In the afternoon I went with all the children swimming in a near-by small pond. Again after dinner Paul and I talked on the front porch till close to midnight. In the afternoon we set up the nylon mountain tent, and Mathias slept in it in a sleeping bag. Alice very quickly got the hang of a wood-burning kitchen range and the kitchen, and we soon established a system for big eating. Karen was especially delighted with a "fwing" in one of two fine apple trees a short distance in front of the cottage. Mathias put up the old tent between the two trees. Esther got a saw horse from behind the house, had me carry it to these trees, and with much climbing, swinging, and tenting the children made great use of the apple trees.

Monday, July 29.—I woke before 6 (in a sleeping bag), saw the sun rise, built fires, and immediately after breakfast pitched in to "settling"—changing things around to make room and helping Alice to get things in order. Before I was through, Alice and Carolyn with all the children but Mathias and Mary were off to North Creek on a shopping and foraging expedition. On the way back they visited some falls on Garnet Creek, I believe, and, when the motor got hot coming up from Bakers Mills, fixed and ate lunch in a shady place. They were all waiting (with dinner ready) at close to 7 when Paul, Mary, Mathias, and I returned from a 12-mile trip we started at 11.30 as soon as I had "settled." We climbed up the hill beyond the cottages over a low pass north of Eleventh Mountain along a trail rather overgrown (the nettles bothersome) for a couple of miles, then bushwacked to Mud Pond, deepened by a fine beaver dam. On the way Paul, who of course was ahead, saw a long-earred owl and two deer. At one place we went through a gathering of chickadees and towhees. We saw white wood sorrel in blossom and the closed gentian and the brilliant red berries in clusters of ____ and the large glistening purple-blue berries of ____. But mainly what we saw was the great woods itself. At Mud Pond we stopped at a small peninsula. Paul built a fire while Mary, Mathias, and I got ready for a swim. I swam over to a floating island by a beaver house and brought back in my mouth a plant of ___ to show them, but the water had so many treacherous tangles of down trees submerged by the beaver's raising the water level that I did not have the children come in beyond the submerged edge of the large rock on which we entered. There Mathias swam rings around me, and Mary enjoyed a coyness with the water. We toasted pork sandwiches that Paul had brought, ate a can of grapefruit, ate two oranges apiece, and made away amongst us with a box of graham crackers while drinking the pond. I think I ate most of the crackers. Then we bushwhacked to Second Pond Flow—a wide expanse of high grass growing in bunches—higher than Mathias's head in some places. He and Mary crept through the grass as we stayed there a bit. And we all lay and watched fish in the stream that meanders through this grassy wide plain which looks like a lake of grass. Then we started home and had a trail to follow all

the way. It was a great first-day taste of the Adirondacks, and part
of its refreshment was in knowing that when we were at the wildness
of Mud Pond (Paul doubted that anyone had been there since he was
there last fall) and at Second Pond Flow, the nearest dwelling or road
was at our cottages to the east, and that the nearest road to the south,
west, or north, was 20 miles away. I wished that I knew the country
well enough to go back there with the family overnight, but shied at
the thought of being in there without trails. After returning I built
a fire in the fireplace, expecting Paul and Carolyn to come over, but
Paul fell asleep as soon as he had eaten, so Carolyn said, and she went
home with her children at bedtime. Karen got into a sleeping bag in
a bunk. Mathias and Esther went to sleep in bags in the tent. Alice
and I enjoyed our own fire until it burned down after midnight, then
ate graham crackers and peaches by candle light. Esther and Karen
had by then crawled out of the sleeping bags (too hot), and I put them
into bed in a bunk together. And Alice and I went to sleep about 1.30.
I think I got as much out of this day as there was in it.

Tuesday, July 30.—We slept till after 7, when Mathias got
around, wrapped up the sleeping bags, and took down and folded the
mountain tent. I got up about 8 and built a kitchen fire and after
breakfast snoozed in the cot I had moved onto the sunny-morning side
of the porch. Paul left for Schenectady but before going went over
some maps with me and suggested how we would use our time. I gave
him $25 with which to buy sleeping bags and film if possible. We got
ourselves organized as to knapsacks, bathing suits, and the lunch
(packed by Alice) and drove up to the Putnam farm at the southwest
(well up) Crane Mountain, guided there by O'Kane's *Trails and
Summits of the Adirondacks*, our family (except Edward) and Mary.
At the Putnam's we saw a baby that reminded us lovingly of Edward—as something or other keeps doing. We climbed a steep, very
satisfying trail with good outlooks to Crane Mountain Lake. There
we all swam, I building a fire while the rest dressed and started the
swim. As Alice came to spread the lunch, I went for one of the best
swims I have had. Then we toasted our sandwiches, ate, and rested.
Instead of climbing to the summit, we swam again—until clouds,
some wind, and distant thundering led us to prepare to leave. But

we didn't go immediately. Karen went fishing with a hookless, poleless line, as Alice sunned herself. The rest of us walked around the lake, in a few places going up the mountain side a ways for a view and "exploration." In some places we had no trail and except for the lakeside where the summit trail is the area seemed little frequented. We heard the hermit thrush beautifully (as we ate lunch we heard and listened for the full, thin song of the whitethroat) and we ate many blueberries. Back to Alice and Karen, we made up our packs and started down. Mathias carried all the bathing suits (except for Mary's; she had her own neat back basket) both up and down. Esther made the hike both ways unaided. Going up I carried the big knapsack with food and held Karen's hand, two or three times swinging her up and over hard places, while she climbed the whole ascent. Alice carried the knapsack down, while Karen rode my back most of the way but walking down also a good bit. As we came down to the Putnam's farm and looked down on a field of new-mown hay where all hands were at work with rain coming on, we were delighted to see the baby (afar off) sitting in a stack of hay potting away with his hands flying high. It was as lovely a thing as we had seen. We drove on down the mountain—a hard two miles either way—and arrived home about 6.30, for a dinner Alice quickly fixed with hamburg and certain trimmings. Alice wrote cards and I wrote this journal from the beginning to this point, retiring a little before midnight. (While Alice got dinner this day I read to M, E, & K. from Padraic Colum's *The Children of Odin*.)

Wednesday, July 31.—After the fires were made, the breakfast eaten, the water carried, and other morning chores out of the way, Karen went with Carolyn and girls to visit George Morehouse and wife, Alice packed a lunch, the rest of the children played, and I read in J. T. Headley's *The Adirondacks; or, Life in the Woods* and studied some maps. About 11 o'clock I packed the lunch in the sugar sack with sweat shirts, Mathias and I packed a knapsack with water, Mary put oranges in her pack basket, and with Esther we started south across the fields (saw a pale blue crayfish and some trout in a meadow brook) to the high point of fields on the eastern slope of Eleventh Mountain, marked by a couple of dead trees, and then bushwhacked westward up the mountain, keeping south of a ravine and heading for the only lookout rock visible from our cabin. For a great distance we could see little from the tall undergrowth we went through and I was busy with my walking stick and leather boots breaking a way through down branches [so] that Esther (immediately behind me) could get through. Near the top we went more easily through spruce, though the sharp dead lower branches (in many places intertwined) were annoying to me. Before we reached the top we had to clamber up large rocks. Going up one of these I frightened a bird that flew so suddenly I suspected a nest. I hardly knew what the bird was. But I found the nest deep in the moss on the edge of the rock under a seedling spruce. There were three young in it, and I took some pictures. As it later developed we came out pretty close to the lookout we were seeking, it being only a short ways to our left. Mary, who had been up before but a long time ago, thought it was to our right. So we started looking for it there—a very difficult rock to find because close enough to be seen by us it was fairly well concealed by trees. We enjoyed a couple of other outlooks and then ate on a large flat rock on top of the ridge, the sun coming out on this rainy day just as we finished and were ready to sprawl. We went on up the ridge and over to the west side to look out there and then back down the ridge part way down the east side until we found the lookout and stood on it—seeing Gore Mountain and looking down on our cabin. Seeing the car gone, I knew Alice had gone shopping and I was glad. This was my father's birthday anniversary, and before leaving I had written to my mother. I knew Alice would mail the letter. We bushwhacked down the mountain again and came out at the same rock we stood on to cross the fence in leaving the field for the woods. We idled along, eating red raspberries, watching trout in the meadow brook, and enjoying a light rain. We arrived back shortly after Alice, Carolyn, and the younger children had returned. We felt good and had no mishaps except that Esther had been twice stung by yellowjackets as we were exploring the top of the ridge. Esther discovered a large snake and Mary and Mathias saw it, but I did not. As Alice had started up the mountain from Bakers Mills the car motor got too hot to go on, so they all stopped in a shady place and made up a lunch from their shoppings. I drove down to Bakers Mills after dinner to

Lunch stop en route to the Adirondacks at Gettysburg, Pennsylvania on Friday, July 26. From left, Mathias, Esther, Karen and Alice.

Paul Schaefer's parents' cabin, named Cragorehol after Crane, Gore, and Height of Land mountains. See Saturday, July 27.

Carolyn Schaefer at their 100-year-old log cabin, Echo Lodge, where Carolyn played the violin to a near-full moon on Saturday, August 10.

Paul Schaefer and John S. "Appie" Apperson, his conservation mentor, near Lake George on Saturday, August 3. Appie's boat was named Article XIV Section 1 *for the "forever wild" section of the New York State Constitution.*

Paul Schaefer photo

Zahnie and Mathias, with the Schaefer family minus the baby Monica, climbed Crane Mountain from the Putnam Farm on Sunday, August 4. Paul, Zahnie (shown here), and Mathias climbed to the summit.

On the High Peaks trip on August 8 and 9, Zahnie, Paul, and Ed Richard set up camp here at the Flowed Lands lean-to.

Departure day meant group pictures, Sunday, August 11: From left, Mathias, Evelyn, Francis "Cub," Esther, Karen, and Mary in front of Zahnie, Alice, Carolyn, and Paul on the porch swing at Cragorehol. After picture taking, Paul and Zahnie walked up onto Height of Land where Zahnie first saw the cabin belonging to Harold and Pansy Allen that the family would purchase.

Ed Zahniser was not along on the 1946 trip. He and Zahnie are perched atop one of the children's favorite play rocks at Mateskared about 1950.

Mateskared, the Zahniser cabin named after Mathias, Esther, Karen, and Edward, as it was when Zahnie sat at the front right window drafting Wilderness Bill language in the late 1950s and early 1960s.

see about the motor but found out nothing and had no trouble with it on my return (in the coolness of evening). I slept nicely this rainy night in a sleeping bag on a cot on the porch, after reading Keat's "Sleep and Poetry" and several other poems before the fireplace.

Thursday, August 1.—On this rainy day, it rained. About 11 o'clock we started in two cars (Nat had come back with his Plymouth during the night) and drove to North Creek and after some shopping continued on a tour that took us north through Minerva to Newcomb, west to Indian Lake, Deerland, Blue Mountain Lake, Racquette Lake, back east and southeast to Indian Lake, south then to Speculator, and on around east and north to Bakers Mills, at about 11 p.m. Soon after we left North Creek a downpour started and in our car we sang and told stories. I remember that I told guess-who stories of Samson, St. Francis of Assisi, and Theodore Roosevelt. (We had just passed near the place where Roosevelt became president.) At Deerland we followed the Racquette River down to Forked Lake. We saw a 2-canoe portage along the road here, and when we came to the road end saw a fisherman with about a 3 1/2-pound brook trout and several others. He gave us 2 rainbow trout. Two campers Mathias and I talked with told us they had seen (and heard) a loon on Forked Lake. They offered us their campfire, but Carolyn had already started one in a nice place under some trees offering fair shelter from the rain. We ate frankfurters, bananas, and milk mainly. Back along Racquette River we saw the Buttermilk Falls after some confusion in finding them and for some time watched their wild whiteness over the black rocks. There were brilliant cardinal flowers on the far shore. Blue Mt. Lake was beautiful and it was not too rainy while we were there. At Racquette Lake (the lake, not the town) where we turned around we saw canoeists and watched a herring gull. Perhaps the best part of the day was our trip southward along Indian Lake. At the crossing of the link between Indian Lake and Lewey Lake, Nat had to change a tire, and the rest of us made a sort of dinner on graham crackers, peaches, left-over frankfurters (cooked but cold), and raisins. The children and I enjoyed walking out along Indian Lake and seeing several tent camps. From there on south we were on a dirt road with miles of wilderness on either hand, our own camp the nearest "civilization" to the east and it 20 miles across the wilderness that we had just tasted on Monday. At one place Alice spied a deer that stood while we backed the car and watched it. This dirt road seemed wilderness itself. When we got back to camp we were all so tired we simply went to bed.

Friday, August 2.—Mathias was up about 8 and made the fires with only a little help from me at the end. We were all late getting around, and it was about 10 before we ate. While Alice cleaned up the breakfast and packed lunches, I "red up" and swept and cut wood and carried water. Mathias read "Robin Hood" aloud after I had read a couple of chapters aloud yesterday or day before to him, E. & K. About 11.30 we all (in 2 cars) headed for Gore Mt. via North Creek (where we did a little shopping) and the best mountain road I have known, leading up to the garnet mine and made of garnet-mine materials. We left the cars at the mine and made the hike to the summit, eating (in the rain) at a fire Carolyn made along the trail— soup, eggs, a bit of bacon, and peaches. Nat initiated one of our Boy Scout cooking kits by frying the rainbow trout we got yesterday (for Carolyn et al, who could eat no meat) and I initiated the other by frying two eggs with a bit of bacon for myself. But the most of the cooking was in a big skillet. The top of Gore Mt. was wonderfully luxuriant and moist, and at its south end where there is a good lookout about a cliff or sharp gulf the sun came out beautifully as we looked across to Crane Mt., Height of Land, Eleventh Mt., and the wilderness to the west of our camp. We could not quite see our camp, but we could see the lookout rock where we were Wednesday and almost all the field we had traversed in getting to its woods. I took several pictures. Mathias and Evelyn saw a deer on their way up. Esther and Karen had a good time watching a bright golden-brown toad (American toad). Karen walked all the way up, but I carried her nearly all the way down. Mathias, Esther, Karen, and I stayed together on the way down, and I enjoyed it very much. Back at the car, we found it about 6 o'clock. We drove home, Mathias and I built a fire and got water, Alice fixed a dinner in a hurry, and we ate peas, potatoes, and wheat-muffin cereal with peaches. The children went right to bed. I wrote in this journal from Wednesday morning to this point. (Nat, Carolyn, and their children all had to go down to Schenectady tonight, not knowing just when they would return. Paul had not come back.)

Saturday, August 3.—Paul's truck was here. So as soon as we were up and about I walked over to his cabin (about 8.30) and invited him over for breakfast. Mathias had built the kitchen fire alone. His interest and pride were shown by his disappointment as it died down. We found that he had put too large a log on the kindling and soon had it going well. While I busied myself about at little things I talked with Paul, and Alice worked in the kitchen and got lunch. Archie (Bobcat) Ranney and his visiting son came over to the porch and with Paul talked on the porch and told yarns. Mr. Ranney sang some of his mountain ballads, and I read aloud some of Martha Keller's *Brady's Road and Other Ballads*. After lunch we with Paul drove over to Bolton Landing, there met J. S. Apperson at his camp and were soon in his Chriscraft, *Article XIV Section 1*, seeing Lake George. Mathias, Esther, and Karen were delighted. The wild end of the lake and the islands are certainly precious wild areas—especially to me the Tongue Mt. area. Mr. Apperson, a diplomatic engineer for General Electric, has for years been making the public interest in Lake George preservation his zealous personal concern at the expense of his time and money. He told us of his many experiences. We picked up a canoe at one landing and then anchored off Phenita Island, Paul, "Appie," and I going ashore and seeing the evidence of shore erosion and hearing "Appie" tell about the effects of the high water created by an International Paper Co. dam. What he told about the natural dam was very interesting; it seemed to me that a record of his long efforts and an explanation of Lake George features would make an excellent article. On the way back we looked at a number of islands, especially Dome Island, which Mr. Apperson owns and is holding to turn over to any agency or person or group that will be able to see that the island remains as it is—wild, without buildings, but available for camping to "the little fellows." I wondered if this might not be a good Wilderness Society project and Paul thought so when I asked him later. He thought that perhaps Apperson was throwing out that suggestion. To Mr. Apperson I said nothing about this, however. Back at his boat landing we had a cold, cold swim—wonderfully refreshing—in Lake George, where we could stand and see our toes—so clear was the water. I offered Apperson any possible help in his efforts, and he gave me some of his recent mailings. Perhaps we could publish an article reporting the island erosion findings of Dr. John Lamb, H. H. Wilson of the Soil Conservation Service and A. F. Gustafson of Cornell. We ate dinner in Warrensburg on our way back and then met five women of the Adirondack Mt. Club who had just spent 2 weeks over by Indian Lake and persuaded them to follow us back to our camp. We all ate watermelon. Three of the guests—2 from Bel Air, Md.—stayed with us and 3 at Schaefers. Carolyn and the children were back.

Sunday, August 4.—Alice, Esther, and Karen stayed home—Esther to be chairman of the welcoming committee for Mendal and Edith. Paul, Carolyn, Mary, Evelyn, Cubby, Mathias and I drove over to the Putnam farm and climbed Crane Mt., the baby staying with Alice. On a back road, off our way, we saw a red fox cross the road and run right back. We had a little chat with the Putnams. Mathias and I had a good climb together to the large rock just below the lake, where we sprawled, looked at the view of Garnet Lake and hills and waited for the others. At the lake we picked blueberries, swam, and ate a lunch—Mathias and I down by the lake with sandwiches that Alice had made. I met a number of Adirondack Mtn. Club members, this being an outing for them. Paul, Mathias and I climbed to the summit and from the tower saw a great view. We went down a northern descent. At the lake we saw 7 speckled trout caught by a fisherman on a raft. Each was about a pound. He also had 3 bullheads. Back down the mt. trail (we looked at a cave en route), we went in the Putnams, had rich, cold milk, saw a beautiful organ! At "home" Alice had a dinner for all of us. Paul, Carolyn, Alice and I sat on the swing talking till Paul had to start for Schenectady. Just then Mendal and Edith made their much expected arrival. We made a fire, got rather settled, and talked till midnight. I slept on the porch in a sleeping bag. There was a heavy rain soon after Mendal and Edith came, lasting into the night, but the day had been beautiful—though too hazy for good views from the mountain.

Monday, August 5.—I saw the sun rise over the hill, was up at 7.30 and after making a fire hiked with Mathias up the road onto Height of Land Mt. to the last house, which is for sale. A great view of Crane Mt. in the distance and of Eleventh Mt. As we came back we heard a breakfast bell and smelled bacon—which Mendal and Edith had brought. I wrote this journal from Sat. a.m. to this point while children played, Mathias piled wood, Mendal fixed things up and played the organ, and Alice and Edith did kitchen work and got ready for a trip to Thirteenth Lake. We went through North Creek, where we shopped, then up the Hudson and into Thirteenth Lake on a woods road. We finally abandoned the cars and walked down what was labeled "Elizabeth Point Trail." It was a beautiful sort of peninsula rather high above the water. I took the children for a swim while lunch was getting under way; after lunch I helped Mary and Mathias fish, then swam some more. Finally about 5 we hiked out to the car. Mathias and I went ahead and cleaned the fish. We had quite a pack train, each with a knapsack of some sort and two of us carrying the baby's basket on a pole. I took some pictures of Mendal and Edith sitting on a large rock just below where we ate. Thirteenth Lake is 1674 feet above sea level, surrounded by good looking hills. Most of it is wild and the small eastern area is appropriately "developed." In the evening we sat about a good fire after the children were abed, Mathias on the porch. (Before dinner I read Robin Hood aloud to Mathias, Esther, Karen, Mary, and Evelyn seated around the fireplace.) We also sat awhile on the porch swing, the half moon just down the back of Eleventh Mt. still making a glow around the top like a corona. We thought we saw northern lights. After still some more talking about the dwindling fire we went to bed about midnight. I slept with Alice in the top bunk above Esther & Karen until I had to get Karen up at 5.30 and then lay in a bag on the porch cot and watched the reddened sunrise sky.

Tuesday, August 6.—While breakfast was being prepared I finished dressing the fish, and the children after breakfast had a fish fry that Carolyn held over their outdoor fireplace—while I shaved (!) and wrote in this journal to this point.

Mendal, Edith, Alice, Mathias, Esther, Karen and I went in our car, the top down, around through North Creek, and up to the Garnet Mine. On the way up we had a hot motor and enjoyed a panorama while it cooled. We had a good fire and lunch in the same place as before. Alice and Karen stayed there, later climbing a ways and returning to the car where Karen took a nap. Alice carried the knapsacks to the car. The rest of us climbed Gore slowly. I missed Alice and Karen, but we all had a good time. We discovered a towhee's nest with 3 eggs, along the trail, under a canopy of moss—in a miniature cave. Near the ranger's cabin Mathias spied a porcupine climbing a pine. Esther was much interested in seeing how trees grow—especially in one small one that was five years old. We went to the southern overlook. Mendal and Edith were interested in the view and the experience, though I doubt that they were much excited by mt. climbing as a sport. Edith, Mendal, Esther & I climbed to the tower, where we enjoyed the view of the high peaks, though I appreciated more the view of Second Pond, Botheration Pond, and the wilderness beyond them. But I don't enjoy climbing towers. I ran all the way down, stopping at the towhee's nest and almost catching the bird. Then I went back up from Alice and the car till I met, Edith, Mendal & Esther and carried Esther the last part of the way. Mathias ran down to and was not far behind me. Back at the cabin we had a good dinner, but did not stay up very late. I slept in a sleeping bag on the porch cot.

Wednesday, August 7.—As soon as breakfast was over I started getting things together for an overnight hike with Mathias, which proved to be about as good an experience as I have ever had. [Marginal note: Just as we were starting, Mr. Ranney came over to talk about Boy Scouts and to give me $1 for a Wilderness Society gift membership for Donald McCarty, 410 June Street, Union District, Endicott, N.Y., a scout master.] I took two sleeping bags, the tent, camera, tripod, glasses, and extra clothing in the new Army surplus ruck sack, with the small axe on my belt. Mathias took all the food, which Alice packed up fine for us, in the middle size knapsack, and carried over his shoulders the two Boy Scout cooking kits. We went bushwhacking up Eleventh Mt. south by southwest to a ledge which we explored and prepared to make accessible by a pleasant trail. I cut out a good many branches and obstructions. Mathias named this Lookout Ledge. We enjoyed leaving our packs off to explore various ways of climbing the ledge. I took a few photographs. Then we bushwhacked south to the top of the mountain, left our packs where we could find them by two handkerchief flags, and a blazed tree between which and the flags we cleared a visibility lane, and went over to the lookout rock east and took pictures. Then we meandered back to our packs and went west along the mountain top till we crossed the ravine and headed up the next "knob." That developed into rock climbing that was too difficult with our heavy packs so we descended a bit and skirted the south side of the mountain till we came to a lovely (and here rare) level spot under a spruce tree along a well defined deer trail. Here we decided to make camp. We left our packs and explored ahead a ways for water but decided to do without and returned to our camp. While Mathias built up a tepee of kindling in a large circle we had cleared in the duff in a hole we had dug down into sand, I put up the tent. While I was setting up the tripod for pictures Mathias cut two forked stakes for a stick across the fire for soup (which we didn't eat because we found that instead of soup we had a can of concentrate requiring lots of water). But we had a good meal of juicy beans with our hardboiled eggs, sandwiches, chocolate bar, and especially enjoyed bananas and four oranges. We burned all the trash—orange and banana peelings—in the fire as we lay around it. We burned sticks only about 18 inches long, which we had cut with the axe, and kept moving them into the center so that our fire could burn itself completely out, there being no water. We found that we were at an excellent lookout ledge to the south and went out there several times, looking across to Crane Mt. and around to the higher parts of Eleventh. Around the campfire I enjoyed very much Mathias's comments. I said "Sam Magee" for him and when he wished we had brought "Robin Hood" along with us to read from I read out of this journal which he seemed to enjoy thoroughly and offered some corrections, which I made. We sat around the fire till there were fine glowing coals (fanned by blowing) and when these were all blackened we thoroughly covered them with earth and while waiting to make sure the fire was gone we sat out on the ledge and looked at the moon and the moonlit scene. Mathias rolled out the sleeping bags in the tent and I put the rest of the stuff in there or under cover. And we crawled in our bags. I think we were as happy as a man and boy could be. Mathias said, remembering his fire, that we should call the place Camp Glowing Coals. So we named it that. We slept very well except that toward morning we got pretty thirsty. Mathias dreamed it was raining hard and that streams of water were running down the rocks around us. In his sleep talking about this he asked me for a cup!! He got me so thirsty that I got out of the tent and drank a raw egg, which had broken. As soon as it was light we broke camp and made up our packs it was—

Thursday, August 8.—We retraced our steps to the ravine then bushwhacked down it intending to have breakfast by the run on the way home if Schaefer and Ed Richard had not come for me. I had arranged to have a white flag run up the pole if they had come, and when I saw the white flag we hurried on to camp and arrived there in time to have breakfast with the others—about 8 a.m. it was. I felt fine but tired and wringing wet with sweat, and dew. Bushwhacking down that ravine through tall undergrowth that hid the rocks and holes and the down timber was rough going. But Mathias's happiness made it well worthwhile. I laid out my clothes to dry while we packed up for an overnight trip. Alice worked hard to have everything in readiness and about 10 Paul, Ed, and I said goodbyes, and Mendal and Edith drove us way up into the High Peaks region—a wonderful auto trip in itself. I can hardly forget the panorama view from somewhere near North Elba shortly before we turned off Route 86A for Heart Lake, and the view along Cascade Lakes is certainly a rare highway privilege. We had lunch on the way up, and Ed identified a squeak in Mendal's car (which had been bothering him some time) as a broken bearing. He had the wheel taken off and, with a phone call located a bearing assembly that Mendal and Edith could pick up in Saranac after leaving us. We said good-bye to Mendal and Edith at Heart Lake Adirondack Loj, they intending to return to Pa. the next day. I had enjoyed their being with us so much that I was sorry they were going so soon and that I had to be away from them so much while they were up here. They certainly gave us a good send-off for our hike.

Paul, I, and Ed (in our hiking order) started off on one of the best trips I have ever had, in spite of the fact that I had more trouble than ever. I guess the trip with Mathias was not a good preparation. The sciatic nerve in my left hip and leg was excruciating at times, and my pack though much lighter than it was with Mathias did not seem to carry right—a fact that bothered Ed as much as me. So I am afraid I dragged the party a bit. Nevertheless the trip was great. We hiked about 8 miles up a fine trail (Blue) leading first toward the summit of Mt. Marcy till we crossed Marcy Dam, then (Yellow) along Marcy Brook past Avalanche Lake, which is between stupendous cliffs. Looking across it we saw the mass of stone of Mt. Colden at this point with its famous Trap Dyke and at our far end of it saw the debris of the great slide that gives the lake its name. We continued on past Lake Colden, the sun reflected in our eyes and throwing the McIntyre Range across the lake from us (we were along the lake's southeast side) in a beautiful light. We crossed Feldspar Brook at the end of Lake Colden and followed a trail (Red) along the northwest border of the Flowed Lands—and then a little ways up Calamity Brook to a lean-to where we made camp and had dinner [Calamity Brook lean-to]. While Paul and Ed were trying out the fishing I set up the tripod and took some pictures. The roll must have been short, for in winding it I ran it out of the cartridge. After dinner of pork chops, apple sauce, hardboiled egg, toast, coffee and lots of grapefruit juice, we moved our camp over to another lean-to [Flowed Lands lean-to], which had in the meantime been vacated. It is a wonderfully beautifully situated camp at the water's edge, 20 feet or so above the water, looking out through the trunks of spruce, canoe birch, silver birch and across the tops of small spruce, fir balsam, and mountain ash to the McIntyre Range on the left distance and Colden across from it in the right distance and Avalanche Pass in the center distance. I took the film out of the camera in the sleeping bag, only to find that the cartridges of new film did not operate right. More trouble to make the scene seem all the more lovely. We talked in front of the fire and went to sleep in the bags on fir balsam about 11.

Friday, August 9.—After breakfast, while Ed and Paul fished I did various things, of which more later, and wrote in this journal to this point. The "Guide to Adirondack Trails: Northeastern Section," copy of which purchased at Adirondack Loj, shows our route in pencil, gives good restrained descriptions of the country we saw on this trip.

Ed and Paul managed to get a boat but learned that the fishing was not much good—except from 8 to 10 p.m. as someone told them. I took all the dishes down to the water and washed them, using one side of a log as wash and the other as rinse water. Then I washed out some socks on which broken eggs had been soaking. All of which was mainly a means of sitting down by the water in my shorts and watching dragon flies, butterflies, and frogs. The sun felt good on my skin. I took a bath but did not feel like swimming. Then I worked out the trouble with the camera cartridge and got it loaded—successfully as it turned out. By the time Paul and Ed returned I had written the journal up to this day. Then we started down to the outlet of Flowed Lands—the Opalescent, Paul and Ed with fishing rods and I with tripod, camera, and fieldglasses. We walked along the shore, and down the gorge to Hanging Spear Falls. This meant going down a cliff some distance below the falls and at the gorge bottom walking back up the stream to the falls. I doubt that very many people get there. Two places, we had to walk in rather small niches along the cliff, Paul showing the way and taking my tripod ahead of me. Ed tried to make me feel comfortable in not going farther, but we went on. Ed fell in one place about to his hips. First I knew of it I saw him lying on his back with his feet in the air, draining. We took a good many pictures of the falls and found the fishing no good, then returned. As I came along on the cliffs on the return, Paul took no chance of my slipping but reached over after he had crossed, took me on his shoulders, and carried me the couple of steps out of danger. Then up the cliff again back along the same route to the lean-to, a meal, more dish-washing by the lake, and some final picture taking. We left by returning to Calamity Brook and going down it. We saw the monument to Henderson, well described by Paul as like the stone a well-to-do local family would erect in a small town cemetery. At Calamity Pond Ed and Paul tried futilely their final fishing. The trail then down Calamity Brook and out was just fine, slightly down hill most of the time. We were on the trail to Henderson Lake, but where it turns off to the N.W. away from the brook we continued on to the West along the brook, or by then the Upper Hudson on Henderson, until we came out of the wilderness—at Adirondack Village (where naturalist John Burroughs once stayed). About 1 1/2 miles down a dirt road Alice, Mathias, Karen, and Evelyn were waiting for us with Ed's car. IT WAS GOOD TO SEE THEM. When we got back to Cragorehol we found that Carolyn had dinner for all of us. I had a good discussion with Ed and we all talked till Paul and Ed had to go. Alice and I went to bed rather early. The trip had been great but it also was good to be back home.

Saturday, August 10.—It was good being around the cottage all day, packing and loading and helping Alice get the cabin ready for the Schaefer's arrival. There was a heavy downpour when we woke up. I had to run out and put the top of the car up. Then a struggle for fires. All morning between showers I was putting our old tent out to get it dry for packing. Alice and Carolyn went to town and I took care of the children. Late in the afternoon Gene and Gertie Morehouse fixed the car's distributor for us. After dinner (late) all the children, ours and the Schaefers's too, gathered in front of our fireplace and I read the Robin Hood chapter describing the King's archery contest, the last part by flashlight. That was a cozy picture of children to remember. After the children were in bed Alice and I sat on the front porch swing and watched the near-full moon above Crane Mountain. Then Carolyn—over at Echo Lodge—began to play the violin. That was wonderful, and the clouds going across above Crane Mountain under the moon were beautiful. Then across Eleventh Mountain layer clouds came. Alice went over and sang a bit with Carolyn, and I kept on watching the clouds. Alice returned and we sat up till Mr. and Mrs. Peter A. Schaefer [parents of Paul Schaefer] came with their son Carl and his two boys. We turned the camp over to them. All our things were packed and we all slept in our sleeping bags—I on the front porch on the cot. Last of all in the day Paul came back up from Schenectady and he and I talked till after midnight.

Sunday, August 11.—I did the final chores around, readying the camp for successors and prepared to take group pictures. I let Paul take our car to go in to North Creek to mass. When he returned he said I still owed him 30 minutes. So I left with him on a tramp up over Height of Land Mountain back down through Harold Allen's place where we looked at the view of Crane Mt. and talked. [The next year Howard and Alice Zahniser bought the Harold Allen place at the top of Edwards Hill Road and named it Mateskared, for the four children.] By the time we got back we had been gone about 3 hours. Paul's brother Vincent (with wife Lois and children) was there then briefly and I met and talked with them. Vincent knows Bernard Frank [a forester and founder of The Wilderness Society]. As soon as I could eat and we could get our final little packing done we started away with a good send-off from all the Schaefers—about 3 p.m.

We drove on Route 8 with the top down to Piseco Lake and there stopped at the Pt. Comfort campgrounds. The children and I went to swim a bit after I built a fire. Then Alice cooked a dinner of canned meat, baked beans, tomatoes, peaches, coffee, etc. We watched our fireplace awhile and saw the full (I think) moon rise over and reflect across Piseco Lake. Karen went to bed there in a sleeping bag in the backseat. The rest of us drove on in the moonlight (There were here and there clouds or layers of fog to go through) until about 3 miles north of Cold Brook (as the odometer showed the next morning). I pulled off the road at a likely looking spot and fixed up a camp on the ground. Esther slept on the front seat, Alice, Mathias and I on the ground. I spread the old tent and two car blankets out under our sleeping bags. We lay and watched the stars in the moonlight, later the clouds, and northern lights. Some time about then it was—

Monday, August 12.—As soon as we got around we drove on to Utica and had breakfast there in a diner. There we took Route 5 to Chittenango and then Route 13 to Horselands (north of Elmira) where we picked up Route 17 and followed it to Redhouse and then came on down the Allegheny to Tionesta [Pennsylvania]. The Chittenango Falls along Route 13 seemed interesting and the area a convenient place to camp overnight. It was a beautiful, sometimes cloudy day, with good views of the hill country of central N.Y. and of the hills along the southern border of N.Y.—looking like Pennsylvania hills. At Quaker Bridge we saw by chance Olive Fenton and went with her to her house where we chatted a moment with her and Bill [ethnologist William Fenton]. At a designated picnic ground in the Allegheny National Forest about 4 miles up the river we cooked a dinner of ham and eggs and scotch broth with lots of vegetables and had some cabbage. Toward dusk we headed on to Tionesta and on the way bought some ice cream which we ate with Mother [Bertha Belle Newton Zahniser] and Aunt Luella [Newton] before going to bed in a bed—though the children were on the floor and still in sleeping bags.

Tuesday, August 13.—I wrote in this book August 9 on at Mother's house in Tionesta and prepared to get back to Washington [D.C.] the next day. The journal as a record of activities ends here.

Zahnie at Hanging Spear Falls, August 1946.

To Hanging Spear Falls
With Zahnie

By Paul Schaefer

Hanging Spear Falls and the Opalescent River climax the wildest and most spectacular river source in the Adirondack Mountains. Near the heart of the High Peak wilderness, this crystal clear stream is a beginning of the majestic Hudson River which rises on Mount Marcy about five miles upstream and 2,000 feet higher than the falls.

The Hanging Spear, which is the final drop of a cataract about six hundred feet high, epitomizes the wild character of New York State's 2,600,000-acre Forest Preserve. Above the cataract is a lovely sheet of water called the Flowed Lands at elevation 2,763 feet above the sea. To understand elevations in the Adirondacks, it is well to keep in mind the fact that Lake Champlain, which borders the Park for more than one hundred miles on the east, is but 93 feet above sea level. Mount Marcy, less than 25 miles away, rises 5,251 feet above this lake.

Close by the Flowed Lands is Livingston Pond, deep and dark, bordered by virgin cedars. A short distance easterly is Lake Colden, and another half mile away is Avalanche Lake. These three mountain lakes, totaling over two miles in length, are hemmed in by precipitous four- to five-thousand-foot peaks. Virgin spruce and other evergreens heavily clothe the lower slopes, gradually diminishing in size, until on the higher elevations they run into alpine conditions above timberline.

On August 8, 1946, Howard Zahniser, Edmund Richard, and I shouldered our packs at Heart Lake, which is in the valley not too far from Lake Placid, and headed up the steep trail to Avalanche Pass on the way to our destination—the Hanging Spear. Zahniser, or Zahnie as he was often called, was then Executive Secretary and Editor of The Wilderness Society. We had met for the first time several months earlier at the National Wildlife Conference in New York City, where we had presented a pictorial program designed to help save the Moose

River from destruction by Higley Mountain and Panther Mountain dams. The lights had scarcely been turned on after the presentation when Howard introduced himself and Carl Gutermuth—he himself pledging editorial support in *The Living Wilderness*, and Gutermuth pledging financial support, in our effort to preserve the Moose River. Howard indicated a strong desire to see the Adirondacks, and then and there we had made plans for such a trip. And this was it.

As we eased our packs onto great blocks of stone which cluttered the pass at Avalanche Lake, it was an hour later and we were a thousand feet higher. Cliffs of great mountains rise sharply from this narrow cleft and the clarity of echoes here is almost startling.

The trail is very rough in this area: it goes under, over, and around the huge chunks of cliffs broken from above. At this point Ed, who is an Adirondack guide, successfully complained of light-footedness and convinced us both to let him tote an unequal load. "I've just got to get in shape for carrying deer this fall," he said. And like most guides (despite a background of college and successful business), he spat tobacco to emphasize his point.

It was a fine experience for me to be walking down spruce and balsam trails with men like Zahnie and Ed. The falls were really not more of an objective than every foot we were traversing. For this was the Adirondack Forest Preserve—one of the most spectacular parts of it. This particular section contains about 250,000 acres of the Preserve, including dozens of peaks exceeding 4,000 feet, many lakes, and the sources of numerous rivers.

Our conversation, from the time we started up the trail until about dark, was almost entirely about wilderness. We discussed the genesis of the Adirondack Park by the young Albany engineer and explorer, Verplanck Colvin, who dreamed it in 1868; and we discussed its development up through the years to the Constitutional Convention of 1894. By a vote of 122 to 0, the delegates of that convention wrote into the State Charter those inimitable words which have so magnificently protected the Adirondacks since that time: "The lands of the state, now owned or hereafter acquired, constituting the forest preserve as now fixed by law, shall be forever kept as wild forest lands."

We discussed the almost constant attacks made upon this article by commercial interests, seeking water power, timber, or other resources. All of the major attacks had been repulsed, usually by an overwhelming vote of the people. Zahnie was amazed to learn that for the first 37 years of the constitutional protection, the people of the City of New York almost single-handedly maintained the integrity of the Forest Preserve. Time after time, upstate New York voted for commercializing the public lands: time after time the plurality of the metropolitan vote overcame and defeated the proposed exploitations. In 1932 the trend of upstate voting changed and since then it has maintained its strong support of the "forever wild" clause.

Zahnie was steeped in the early adventures of Bob and George Marshall and the tradition of wilderness preservation they brought from New York to Washington. Now he began to realize the depth of their commitment and why they so vigorously championed the wilderness. He had not realized the vastness and the extent of the wild forest country of the Adirondacks; nor had he realized the size of the Park, which exceeds in size the State of Massachusetts.

I had known Zahnie's predecessor, Robert Sterling Yard, Editor of *The Living Wilderness*, and I was, of course, very much interested in the man who was to carry the torch lit by Bob Marshall. I think Ed Richard aptly described our first reaction to Zahnie when, soon after we had started this trip, he remarked to me on the side, "He sure can ask questions!" Zahnie asked good, penetrating questions that got right to the root of the matter and was not satisfied with a half answer. We both felt that he had a patience built on impatience. "We can save the significant parts of the American wilderness," he said, "if we don't waste time doing it."

We had hardly mentioned our main Adirondack battle during the day—the threat that Higley Mountain and/or Panther Mountain dams would destroy the Moose River wilderness. But we got to it that night. Ed and I had initiated the fight about a year and a half earlier, after I had been alerted to the threat by George Marshall in New York City. These reservoirs would penetrate to the heart of an area of nearly 1,000 square miles unbisected by road. At that time much of it was private land; today, a great deal more of that country has been acquired by the state. It is a land of forests and lakes, with few high mountains, and has wonderful habitat for wildlife, especially the deer. What we needed now was nationwide support—the kind of support that Bob Marshall had in mind when he helped to found The Wilderness Society.

As a matter of fact, within five miles of our campfire, on Mount Marcy's summit, Bob had voiced words to me in 1932 which became an indelible part of my thinking. He said: "We simply must band together—all of us who love the wilderness. We must fight together— wherever and whenever wilderness is attacked. We must mobilize all of our resources, all of our energies, all of our devotion to the wilderness." And here, under a starlit sky in the very shadow of that mountain, was one who, like Bob Marshall, was a wilderness pre- server in his own right, suggesting national strategy to help us in our efforts to save the Adirondacks.

A whole new battle to preserve the south branch of the Moose River began that night. No longer would a handful of New Yorkers be pitted alone against the most powerful commercial interests in their state. Now there were also people like Dr. Ira Gabrielson and Carl ("Pink") Gutermuth of the Wildlife Management Institute; Anthony Wayne Smith, then Chief Counsel and Chairman of the Conservation and Development committee of the CIO; David Brower, then of the Sierra Club; Devereux Butcher, then of the National Parks Association; and many others who would forcefully join the fray. And they did! All that Zahnie said he would do he did, and so much more that it can never be equated!

Today, more than 20 years later, the south branch of the Moose River still flows unobstructed down through lovely avenues of ancient evergreens; the Indian River still adds its tribute to the Moose through banks of fern by its still waters; the deer still have their winter yarding grounds on the fabled Moose River plains, where all was to have been transformed into cemeteries of stumps and dreary mud flats!

About 10:30 we stopped talking about wilderness and just soaked it in. Shadows from our blazing campfire flickered and danced on the trees around us; occasionally an owl hooted off in the woods, and a warm breeze from the south brought us the sound of the falls of the

Hanging Spear. We reminisced about other such campfires and made plans for more like this. The full richness of Zahnie's personality came into our lives there: the smile that began in his eyes, the faith in his and our cause, his family happiness, and his almost limitless reservoir of friends concerned with our American heritage—we now became a part of all this. The day had been long and rewarding, the morrow would soon be here. . . .

We were awake at dawn and from our sleeping bags we watched the sun fire the 5,100-foot peak of Algonquin and gradually light the evergreens downward to the lake. It was to be another perfect day, when the momentous things of life were again to be the joy of good friends on the trail, the music of water lapping a wild shoreline, the chatter of a red squirrel, and stillness accentuated by the occasional song of a thrush or veery, or the shrill cry of a hawk wheeling high in the sky above us.

After breakfast we went down the trail in back of camp toward Hanging Spear Falls. This is extremely wild and dramatic country. Parallel to the rapids and whitewaters above the final and highest falls, the trail pitches steeply down through spruces and balsams. A sharp bend in the trail revealed a ledge from which a fine view of the falls could be seen from well above it. We made our way down to its base and the great pool there. Zahnie enjoyed the wild splendor of the scene—the solitude, the remoteness, the roar of water, the jumble of cliffs clothed with ferns and mosses and with evergreens clinging to narrow ledges and crannies in the rocks. And in the center of this dark gorge were the sun-drenched falls, sparkling with crystal clear water fed by our most elevated mountain lakes and springs. "How absolutely fitting are these place names," he remarked: "the Hanging Spear, on the Opalescent River."

We tarried at length there, luxuriating in the warm sunshine, feeling the texture of these most ancient rocks and enjoying the lushness of the ferns and mosses and occasional flowers. We spoke very little there, and when it was time to leave, we did so most reluctantly.

Back at the lean-to we enjoyed our final meal. Then Zahnie went down to the water's edge and sat in the sun with his feet in the water. After a while I joined him. "I've been trying to make a comparison of this view to some other one I know," he said, "but there's nothing else I've ever seen quite like it. It has the same kind of perfection I have sensed when looking at the Grand Teton." And then, getting up, he looked once again up the valley towards Avalanche Pass. "So this was Bob Marshall's country," he remarked. "No wonder he loved it so!"

We packed and started our five-mile hike down Calamity Brook toward the historic Tahawus Club, a small cluster of darkly stained summer homes, tucked about a dozen miles up in the woods at the end of the road, occupied by descendants of the early explorers. We passed Calamity Pond, where one of these men accidentally shot himself nearly a century before. Several hours later we reached the Henderson River and Ed's car, driven by Mrs. Zahniser, who had agreed to meet us at the end of our 15-mile hike, at a spot which was more than 60 miles by road from our starting place.

Happily for us, he fell in love with the country and soon had a cabin situated on an east-facing mountain slope close to the Siamese Ponds wilderness. Located at the end of the road, overlooking Crane Mountain and the east central Adirondacks, it was a haven for him and his family which he came to as frequently as possible, to rest from exhausting forays in Washington. Here he could dream a little and plan new strategies for the protection of wilderness. He could also take a trail from his back door and immediately be in a block of State Forest Preserve comprising more than a hundred thousand acres, replete with splendid forests, fifty lakes, innumerable streams and waterfalls, and all that goes to make up land protected from the commercial incursions of man.

I was privileged to have many hours with him here and in the nearby wilderness. We climbed numerous mountains from which we could see thousands of square miles of the Adirondacks, as well as the Green Mountains beyond Lake Champlain, the high peaks about forty miles north, and, on very clear days, Canada beyond the St. Lawrence River to the north, and the Catskill Mountains a hundred miles to the south.

One of his conversations with Ed and me on the trip was most significant in light of future events. He said, "In addition to such protection as national parks and monuments are now given, we need some strong legislation which will be similar in effect on a national scale to what *Article XIV, Section 1*, is to the New York State Forest Preserve. We need to reclaim for the people, perhaps through their representatives in Congress, control over the wilderness regions of America."

Twenty years later, thanks largely to his dedication and indefatigable spirit, this dream became a reality. On September 3, 1964, the President of the United States affixed his signature to the Wilderness Act, which automatically protected a little more than nine million acres of our most cherished lands. Significantly, the President presented the pen with which he had signed the Act to Mrs. Alice Zahniser, whom he had called to Washington for the event in the White House rose garden.

In 1950, Zahnie met in Schenectady with New York State conservation-
ists, from left, Dan Foley, New York State Conservation Council; Dan
Hay, Friends of the Forest Preserve; Lloyd Christenson, Friends of the
Forest Preserve; Zahnie; Alfred Green, Schenectady County Conservation
Council; and Michael Petruska, New York State Conservation Council.

New York's Forest Preserve And Our American Program For Wilderness Preservation

By Howard Zahniser

A year ago I read in the New York Daily Mirror an editorial entitled "Our Priceless Wilds." The first paragraph of this editorial—as succinct a statement as I have yet seen on the New York State Forest Preserve—said forcefully: "The single most valuable possession that we, the people of New York State, all 15,000,000 of us, own in common, and hope to maintain for our children and grandchildren 'forever,' is the Forest Preserve—2,179,556 acres in the Adirondacks and 233,714 in the Catskills."

I can add my personal testimony to the value of these New York state wildernesses. My wife and I with our two boys and two girls have for a number of years spent as much of our summers as we could up on the edge of the forest preserve, in Warren County, on a lovely piece of New York State that we are glad to call our own. At the same time, my work as executive secretary of The Wilderness Society and editor of The Living Wilderness has taken me far and away to great and beautiful wilderness areas throughout our country, and I can thus testify with assurance that here, within the practical reach of some twenty millions of people, are some of the loveliest wilderness retreats left in the United States. New York State is protecting, in fact, our largest park in the United States and the one closest to the most people.

Here today, as several times before on various occasions, I am glad to express in behalf of people in all parts of the country, a gratitude to New York State for its service in preserving in the magnificent areas of the Forest Preserve, our scarcest of all resources—wilderness. And with my "thank you" I wish also to convey a deep feeling of the nation-wide interest in the continuing preservation of this wilderness in your forests.

From within our sheltering walls and fast-moving vehicles our American world seems far removed from the wilderness. The wilderness we have "conquered" and from its raw materials have built a civilization in which we have protected ourselves from hardships and freed ourselves to a great extent from many of our natural limitations.

Yet wilderness preservation has certainly become one of our American purposes, an essential part of a distinctively modern movement for the conservation of natural resources—upon which, it is recognized, the survival of our culture depends. The more highly developed our culture has become, the greater our appreciation of wilderness has grown. The more we have enjoyed the ease and security of our civilization, the more also we have valued the hardships and hazards—the adventure—of wilderness excursions. The farther we have come in our programs for managing our world the greater has become our appreciation of the significance to us of the observations to be made in areas where natural processes go on unmodified by man.

As we have thus achieved the opportunity of leisure to enjoy ourselves and reflect on our progress and our destiny, we have come to realize that the wilderness in all its wildness is important to us, and we have determined to preserve it as a resource of health and inspiration, of knowledge and understanding. We have come to realize that we ourselves are creatures of the wild, that in the wilderness we are at home, that in maintaining thus our access to wilderness we are not, as some have thought, escaping from life but rather are keeping ourselves in touch with our true reality, the fundamental reality of the universe of which we are a part. We call it recreation and often, most fortunately, know its deep benefits through simple enjoyment of a good time. Yet so deliberate and calculated has all our living grown that we have come to realize we must be aware of the true meaning of our wilderness if we are truly to preserve its values, must recognize that its essential importance to us is indeed in its wildness.

Henry David Thoreau, who in his essay on "Walking" declared that "in Wildness is the preservation of the World," was one of the first Americans to point out this significance of wilderness and—even in the middle of the Nineteenth Century, before ever the frontier was gone—to argue for wilderness preservation. Why should we not have "our national preserves," asked Thoreau as he concluded one of his essays, "Chesuncook," in *The Maine Woods*, "to hold and preserve" man himself as "the lord of creation—not for idle sport or food, but for inspiration and our own true recreation?" Thoreau perceived, as he wrote in *Walden*, that our life "would stagnate if it were not for the unexplored forests and meadows which surround it," and he emphasized:

"We need the tonic of wildness,—to wade sometimes in marshes where the bittern and the meadow-hen lurk, and hear the booming of the snipe; to smell the whispering sedge where only some wilder and more solitary fowl builds her nest, and the mink crawls with its belly close to the ground. At the same time that we are earnest to explore and learn all things, we require that all things be mysterious and unexplorable, that land and sea be infinitely wild, unsurveyed, and unfathomed by us because unfathomable. We can never have enough of nature. We must be refreshed by the sight of inexhaustible vigor, vast and titanic features, the sea-coast with its wrecks, the wilderness with its living and its decaying trees, the thunder-cloud, and the rain which lasts three weeks and produces freshets. We need to witness our own limits transgressed, and some life pasturing freely where we never wander." First published in the *Atlantic Monthly* in 1858, Thoreau's plea for national preserves was published (posthumously) in *The Maine Woods*, in 1864, the same year in which the United States government made its first provision for what we now recognize as wilderness preservation. The federal government then, by an Act of Congress approved by President Lincoln on June 30, 1864, granted the Yosemite Valley to the state of California upon the condition that it should be "held for public use, resort, and recreation."

Two decades later, by an Act of Congress approved by President Grant on March 1, 1872, Yellowstone National Park was "dedicated and set apart as a public park or pleasuring-ground for the benefit and enjoyment of the people" and provision made for the "preservation, from injury or spoilation of all timber, mineral deposits, natural curiosities, or wonders within said park, and their retention in their natural condition."

The brilliant and significant surveys and studies begun by the young Verplanck Colvin here in New York State's Adirondacks in the 1870's were at this same time leading to the laws and constitutional provisions that before the end of the century had firmly dedicated the Adirondack wilderness to protection by the State, "forever wild."

John Muir in his *Atlantic Monthly* sketches was doing his best "to show forth the beauty, grandeur, and all-embracing usefulness of our wild mountain forest reservations and parks, with a view to inciting the people to come and enjoy them, and get them into their hearts that so at length their preservation and right use might be made sure."

When the National Park Service was established in 1916, under the leadership of Stephen Mather—some two years after John Muir's passing, on Christmas Eve in 1914—there were 14 national parks, besides 33 national monuments, in the national park system, and there had also been established 153 forest reservations, within which were the great wildernesses destined to be preserved as the primitive, wild, wilderness, and roadless areas of the national forests.

From the Southwest, where on August 25, 1924, the "type specimens" of these areas was established by regional administrative action in the Gila National Forest, Aldo Leopold had by the 1920's begun to point out to the nation both the importance—recreational and ecological—of the national forest wildernesses and the growing threats to their persistence.

And by the 1930's when a national policy for wilderness preservation in the national forests had emerged, the great wilderness interpreter and champion from New York, Robert Marshall—forester, thinker, writer, philanthropist, who learned wilderness in the "forever wild" Adirondacks, where with two companions he had been first to climb all 46 of the peaks 4,000 feet high or higher, who had seen also the great western areas of still living wilderness "melting away like the last snowbank on some south-facing mountainside during a hot afternoon in June"—Robert Marshall—had not only written his now classic interpretation, "The Problem of the Wilderness," in the February 1930 *Scientific Monthly*, but had also achieved his position on the staff of the U.S. Forest Service where he was able to contribute so notably to the establishment of areas for preservation and to the formulation of regulations for their protection.

Thus it was by our 1940's, through the influence of such men as Henry Thoreau, Verplanck Colvin, John Muir, Stephen Mather, Aldo Leopold, and Robert Marshall, and the growing sense among many men and women of the enduring importance of wilderness, that we had in fact in our national park system, in our national forests, and in other federal and state areas a great wilderness preservation system.

Through this system of preserved areas, of which the Adirondack and Catskill wildernesses are important units, we now propose to maintain our access to wildness, to what John Muir called "fountains of life." Our great and expanding civilization, we realize, will eventually modify for human exploitation every last area on the earth—except those that through human foresight and wisdom have been deliberately set aside for preservation. Through such a zoning program, nevertheless, we are persuaded, we can insure the existence of a system of wilderness forever. It is not too late. Half a hundred areas in our national park system, six dozen and more areas within our national forests, a few of our national wildlife refuges, certain of our state parks, and other areas within the public domain and on Indian reservations are still wilderness—and in public ownership. Among the most outstanding of all are the Forest Preserve areas in the Adirondack and Catskill Parks here in New York.

These are the remnants of our primeval wilderness which we can, and must, still preserve. Elsewhere we know we can obtain the timber and mineral commodities we need and shall need, find the needed sites for our great dams and reservoirs, build the roads and landing fields for our mechanical travel in the great outdoors, find also the places for our outdoor recreation with the conveniences and facilities we so well contrive, and in short realize all the benefits that we want from a developed country. In our wildernesses we shall see preserved the unmodified wildness of our primeval origins, our natural home—the areas of unspoiled nature where we can not only seek relief from the stress and strain of our civilized living but seek also that true understanding of our past, ourselves, and our world, which will enable us to enjoy the conveniences and liberties of our urbanized, industrialized, mechanized civilization and yet not sacrifice an awareness of our human existence as spiritual creatures nurtured and sustained by and from the great community of life on the earth, of which we are truly a part.

The wilderness character of the Forest Preserve must be guarded with great care—that quality of the wild out-of-doors which is so easily destroyed by roads, by buildings, by the motorized transportation which is so welcome in getting us away from the city but so out of keeping with the unique character of the Forest Preserve. Such intrusions would damage the very thing we seek to protect. Most assuredly these Forest Preserve areas that are being cherished as wilderness must be protected from timber cutting and from all commercial uses. The resources of the wilderness are not commodities for the market. But we must not only protect the wilderness from commercial exploitation. We must also see that we do not ourselves destroy its wilderness character in our own management programs. We must remember always that the essential quality of the wilderness is its wildness.

Wilderness to most of us is, of course, vacation country, thought about for the most part in connection with our resorts to it for relief from our work-a-day world. It is certainly right for us to think so. Yet, as I tried to point our editorially in the Summer 1952 issue of *The Living Wilderness*, deeper and broader than this vacation value, encompassing it, is the importance of wilderness that relates it to our essential being, indicating the understandings which come in its surroundings are those of true reality. So derivative do our lives seem from the wilderness, so dependent do we seem on a renewal of our inspiration from these wild sources, that we wonder sometimes if we could long survive a final destruction of all wilderness. Are we not truly and in reality human essentially as spiritual creatures nurtured and sustained—directly or indirectly— by a wildness that must always be renewed from a living wilderness?

Is it not thus that we can explain the fact that a wilderness vacation is remembered as more than sport, more than fun, more than simple recreation?

Are not these the understandings which give such profound significance to the longer sojourn that a civilized man or woman occasionally spends in a return to wilderness?

All of us who are conscious of wilderness influences and who reflect
on their meanings have had intimations of these profound values.
And occasionally these thoughts, which we have surmised, are confirmed by the testimonies of individuals who, in the midst of our
highly organized, mechanized, urban civilization, have been intimate
with wilderness.

One such testimony is in Martha Reben's book *The Healing Woods*.
Under the title "Wilderness Therapy," a review of this book in our
Summer 1952 issue of *The Living Wilderness* told how Miss Reben,
who was under treatment for tuberculosis in its advanced stages,
read the advertisement of a guide and, responding to it, took up a
"tent life throughout successive seasons in the peaceful Adirondack
wilderness." Concluding *The Healing Woods*, an account of her experiences and her recovery, Miss Reben wrote:

"The wilderness did more than heal my lungs. While it dwarfed me
by its immensity and made me conscious of my insignificance, yet it
made me aware of the importance of being an individual, capable of
thinking and feeling not what was expected of me, but only what my
own reasoning told me was true. It taught me fortitude and self-re-
liance, and with its tranquility it bestowed upon me something which
would sustain me as long as I lived; a sense of the freshness and
wonder which life in natural surroundings daily brings and a joy in
the freedom of beauty and peace that exist in a world apart from
human beings."

This Adirondack wilderness, where Martha Reben found her healing influences and where so many of us have also found healing in
body, mind, and soul, is indeed one of the most important wilderness
areas in the entire nation. That is true not only because it is so
important to the people of New York State, who themselves constitute
such a great part of the nation, but because the Forest Preserve here
is directly important to so many individuals in all parts of our great
country. It is indeed one of the treasures of our nation. Its loss as
wilderness would be felt throughout the nation. Its future service to
our people in affording to them a resource of wildness can be as

significant as has been its part in the history of the movement that has led to the preservation of wilderness as a natural resource of the people. In the same way that the people of California serve the people of New York State in the preservation of their magnificent groves of Redwoods and Big Trees, so likewise do the people of this state serve Californians in the dedication to preservation of these wild forest lands of the Catskills and Adirondacks. Such service, in accordance with our modern social morality, implies also an obligation, and with a due sense (I trust) of propriety I should like thus to emphasize the responsibility that many conservationists outside New York State feel you here in New York have to all of us, for the continued preservation of these wildernesses.

In emphasizing, however, the importance to the entire nation of the wilderness being safeguarded in the Forest Preserve, I wish also to emphasize my appreciation of its distinctive importance to New York State and my conviction that it must continue for its best protection as a wilderness preserved by the constitution

of the State of New York. Having been in the Adirondacks a great deal myself and having discussed very fully and very frankly the problems of the Forest Preserve with its earnest supporters here in New York State, I know how deeply these people feel their interest in the Forest Preserve as a state treasure. Indeed I number myself among them and feel deeply that the preservation of this wilderness is most fortunately a responsibility of the State of New York. It is my conviction that—such is the unity of our nation, such is the nature of our needs for wilderness, and so great the scarcity of our national wilderness resources—that this responsibility is certainly in part a responsibility of New York State not only to its own citizens but also to the entire nation. I know that this sense of responsibility is deeply felt here in New York State too, that citizens here are thinking not only of the attraction for tourists which grows greater year by year as this wilderness lives on in our complicated civilization, but also of the responsible privilege that they have in perpetuating the great Adirondack and Catskill wildernesses.

Inasmuch as it is provided for in the very constitution of the state, the protection "forever wild" of the Forest Preserve has a security that is unique in all our American programs for wilderness preservation.

I thus express the strong sentiment of conservationists throughout the country who wish deeply to see this protection of the wilderness here in New York State continued under the state constitution, strengthened by its lengthening traditions and by the reassertions of its soundness in the face of repeated challenges. It is in this way that the true wilderness character of these priceless areas can best be safeguarded. But I also look upon this policy in New York State as a valuable, significant example for all other states with wilderness resources still available for protection. Indeed it can well be an example likewise for our federal agencies administering lands that include wilderness. The national interest in the protection of the Adirondack and Catskill wildernesses is definitely an interest in their protection by the State of New York as the Forest Preserve under the state constitution.

The concept of the Forest Preserve is one that I know is deeply cherished. It is indeed a noble and brilliant concept. To sense the practical idealism of this concept—this establishment of a Forest Preserve within the Adirondack and Catskill Parks—is to feel a deep admiration and a pride too in the noble realism of the people of the State. Here are these great parks with their intermingled state and privately owned lands. Within their blue-line boundaries there is established a special and unique kind of human land use. Here the public purpose is the preservation of wild forest lands in their unspoiled wildness, in the public interest. Elsewhere the people of New York State, I also recognize, are realizing the similarly great and noble public purpose of providing state park and other recreational areas for the enjoyment of the outdoors developed and improved by all our various kinds of modern conveniences. But within these blue lines the public purpose, in the interest of all the people, of the present and succeeding generations, is the preservation of wild lands in their primitive splendor and beauty.

Within these blue lines there are no conflicting public purposes now, either as regards the handling of the forests or the provision of recreation. There should be no such conflicts. Within these two parks it is reasonable and proper that the State devote its public holdings wholeheartedly to the important purpose of preserving unspoiled wilderness. In other parts of the state, fortunately, there are being generously provided, for the public, those other recreational programs that are so excellent in their place but so inappropriate within these blue lines. That is excellent. But here we have wilderness— uncut, unspoiled, undeveloped, wild forest lands preserved "forever wild."

An impressive aspect of the program that has developed in carrying out and developing this Forest Preserve concept is its recognition of the privately owned lands within the blue lines. Thus, private enterprise meets the needs and convenience of the public and provides for the owners of private lands a happy living.

As time goes on and generation succeeds generation there is thus being realized in and orderly, harmonious democratic fashion the perfection of the Forest Preserve as a perpetuation of these wild lands, with areas in private ownership near and adjacent for the accommodation and assistance of the ever increasing numbers of visitors that will most assuredly be seeking out these wild retreats.

There are, in truth, it must be clearly discerned, excellent public programs now operating outside these Forest Preserve parks which if once established within these blue lines might conceivably encroach on any publicly owned land there; in other words, on the Forest Preserve itself. It is the peculiar function of the Adirondack and Catskill Parks to insure the people of the state against this very possibility, to hold apart these two certain regions within which all the public lands serve a specific purpose—to make certain, in brief, that all the publicly owned lands within these two regions still rich in remnants of primeval America shall be dedicated to this great public purpose of preserving forever these wild forest lands.

Thus there has been developed here in New York State this unique concept of the forest Preserve within these two great state parks devoted to a single, major purpose. This is one of the greatest pioneer zoning programs that has been developed in our great American and modern experience in managing public lands. The Forest Preserve itself is a zone. The Adirondack and Catskill Parks are zones. This whole concept of the Forest Preserve within specially established state parks is New York's own zoning program—its demonstrations of an effective means for so managing lands as to serve specific public purposes—in this instance the preservation of wild forest lands forever wild. . . .

Our civilization—and I like it—is such that only those areas which are deliberately set aside for preservation in their natural state can be expected to remain unmodified. There is still opportunity, I believe, in this country, to meet all our needs and yet know in perpetuity the values of a system of areas preserved for recreation, for scientific and educational studies, and for historical purposes. What is required to realize this opportunity is a careful study of all our needs in every state and throughout the nation, a deliberate designation of areas for preservation, and then a firm policy of protecting such areas against any destructive or inconsistent uses. In the Adirondacks and Catskills, it seems to me, the people of New York State have already accomplished the firm dedication of certain great wilderness areas and have devised an excellent and unique land-use classification for protecting these dedications. Their example to other state and to our federal agencies is significant and important, as is their service to people throughout our country in preserving these wild forest lands for the enrichment of us all. It is a great pleasure for me to feel that I may be helping to encourage the preservation of this heritage, and I do indeed thank you for the privilege of participating in your studies.

This statement before a committee of the New York State Legislature was delivered by Howard Zahniser, then executive secretary of The Wilderness Society and editor of The Living Wilderness, *in Albany, New York in 1953.*

Seeing her at a committee hearing on wilderness legislation, Senator Estes Kefauver asked Esther Zahniser, age 10 (holding magazine), what she thought about wilderness. Her thoughts and experiences went into the official hearing record, making her the youngest person ever to testify before such a committee. This picture of (from left) Edward, Mathias, Zahnie, Esther, and Karen ran in a Washington, D.C. newspaper. Celebrity Esther was allowed to dress up for the late-night photographer on deadline. Her siblings had to be ready for bed.

The Need for Wilderness Areas

Howard Zahniser

In addition to our needs for urban and suburban parks and open spaces, in addition to the need for a country side of rural loveliness, a landscape of beauty for our living and *in addition* to the needs for parkways and parks and well-developed areas for all kinds of outdoor recreation, there is in our planning a need also to secure the preservation of some areas that are so managed as to be left unmanaged— areas that are undeveloped by man's mechanical tools and in every way unmodified by his civilization.

These are the areas of wilderness that still live on in our national parks, national forests, state parks and forests, and indeed in various other categories of land likewise.

These are areas with values that are in jeopardy not only from exploitation for commodity purposes and from appropriation for engineering uses. Their peculiar values are also in danger from development for recreation, even from efforts to protect and manage them as wilderness.

There is a great need that resides in the desires of so many people for wilderness experiences, a need that should certainly be met. There is likewise a practical need for realizing our ideal of preserving for everyone the privilege of choosing to enjoy the wilderness if he or she so wishes.

There is another practical or immediate need in our compulsion to save from destruction whatever is *best*. Some of our strongest determination to preserve wilderness arises from this motive. . . .

I believe that at least in the present phase of our civilization we have a profound, a fundamental need for areas of wilderness—a need that is not only recreational and spiritual but also educational and scientific, and withal essential to a true understanding of ourselves, our culture, our own natures, and our place in all nature.

This need is for areas of the earth within which we stand without our mechanisms that make us immediate masters over our environment—areas of wild nature in which we sense ourselves to be, what in fact I believe we are, dependent members of an interdependent community of living creatures that together derive their existence from the Sun.

By very definition this wilderness is a need. The idea of wilderness as an area without man's influence is man's own concept. Its values are human values. Its preservation is a purpose that arises out of man's own sense of his fundamental needs.

Wilderness to most of us is vacation country, thought about for the most part in connection with occasional good-time escapes from a civilized life which itself somehow or other seems to be "reality." It is usually only after reflection that one perceives the true reality in the wilderness.

It is, of course, not surprising that recreational values are generally understood as representing the dominant importance of wilderness in our modern civilization. Only in a society that produces the erosion of human beings, the wearing away of soul and body and spirit that is so familiar in our modern circumstances, does the concept of recreation appear.

The wilderness represents the antithesis of all that produces these conditions which recreation remedies. It not only provides the kind of recreation most needed by the increasingly large number who seek wilderness, but it also affords the background for the kind of outdoor recreation for which conveniences and accommodations are provided—the frontier where those who do not wish to experience the rigors of wilderness living and travel may still know in some degree the tonic benefits of its wildness.

Recreational values of the wilderness are thus not only intrinsic but also pervasive throughout the outdoor recreation program of a society with the tastes and resources of the United States. Wilderness preservation is a part therefore of a comprehensive recreational program—a very important part of such a program's provision for outdoor recreation—and it is the ultimate resource for that phase of outdoor recreation that ministers to the individual as such.

But wilderness vacations have those overtones that make them more than narrowly recreational. They are more likely to be joyous than merry, more refreshing than exciting, more engrossing than diverting. Their rewards are satisfaction. There is likely to be a seriousness about wilderness recreation and an earnestness among those who seek it. So philosophers of education who describe their goals in such terms as "life adjustment" and "personality development" may find in the wilderness a most valuable resource, and recreational values in such a context become profoundly educational.

Deeper and broader than the recreational value of wilderness, although indeed encompassing it, is the importance that relates it to our essential being, indicating that the understandings which come in its surrounding are those of true reality. Our lives seem so derivative from the wilderness, we ourselves seem so dependent on a renewal of our inspiration from these wild sources, that I wonder sometimes if we could long survive a final destruction of all wilderness. Are we not truly and in reality *human*, essentially, as spiritual creatures nurtured and sustained—directly or indirectly—by a wildness that must always be renewed from a living wilderness?

Is it not with some such understanding as this that we realize the essential importance of our wilderness areas?

Is it not thus that we can explain the fact that a wilderness vacation is remembered as more than sport, more than fun, more than simple recreation?

Are not these the understandings which give such profound significance to the longer sojourns that a civilized man or woman occasionally spends in a return to the wilderness, gaining experiences that so often prove interesting to so many of us?

It is characteristic of wilderness to impress its visitors with their relationship to other forms of life, and to afford those who linger an intimation of the interdependence of all life. In the wilderness it is thus possible to sense most keenly our human membership in the whole community of life on Earth. And in this possibility is perhaps one explanation for our modern deep-seated need for wilderness.

Because we are so well able to do things, we forget that we can do them only because something else is done. We forget that we can continue only so long as other men, other animals, and other forms of life also keep on doing things. We forget that the real source of all our life is not in ourselves, not even in the Earth itself, but more than

90 million miles away, in the Sun. And not one of us is able alone to
live on this great source. We live only as members of a community.

If for a time some of us might seem to do well at the tragic expense
of other life in this community, we can be sure that it would likewise
be at the expense of our children, our grandchildren, and our great-
grandchildren through the generations that might live. For we know
that we can live on in our descendants only if our Earth community
lives on with them. We not only exist but we are immortal on the
Earth only as members of a great community.

These are facts and understandings that have been known to us
only a comparatively short time—through the observations and studies made by our scientists—and not all of us have appreciated them
rightly. It is not long since man thought of himself as the center of
the universe, thought even of the Sun—the very source of all our
life—as a light by day revolving about the Earth. As our new understanding has come—through science—science also has brought us
many other new and wonderful discoveries, and the new knowledge
of what we *are* has been overlooked by many of us in our eagerness
for the new knowledge of what we can *do*. We have become as proud
over what we can *do* as ever our ancestors could have been over
themselves as the center of the universe.

We deeply need the humility to know ourselves as the dependent
members of a great community of life, and this can indeed be one of
the spiritual benefits of a wilderness experience. Without the
gadgets, the inventions, the contrivances whereby men have seemed
to establish among themselves an independence of nature, without
these distractions, to know the wilderness is to know a profound
humility, to recognize one's littleness, to sense dependence and interdependence, indebtedness, and responsibility.

Perhaps, indeed, this is the *distinctive* ministration of wilderness
to modern man, the characteristic effect of an area which we most
deeply need to provide for in our preservation programs.

Thus the most profound of all wilderness values in our modern
world is an educational value.

As the so-called conquest of nature has progressed, men and
women—separated by civilization from the life community of their

origin—have become less and less aware of their dependence on other forms of life and more and more misled into a sense of self sufficiency and into a disregard of their interdependence with the other forms of life with which they—together—derive their existence from the solar center of the universe.

In the areas of wilderness that are still relatively unmodified by man it is, however, possible for a human being, adult or child, to sense and see his own humble, dependent relationship to all of life.

In these areas, thus, are the opportunities for so important, so neglected a part of our education—the gaining of the true understanding of our past, ourselves, and our world which will enable us to enjoy the conveniences and liberties of our urbanized, industrialized, mechanized civilization and yet not sacrifice an awareness of our human existence as spiritual creatures nurtured and sustained by and from the great community of life that comprises the wildness of the universe, of which we ourselves are a part.

Paradoxically, the wilderness which thus teaches modern man his dependence on the whole community of life can also teach him a needed personal independence—an ability to care for himself, to carry his own burdens, to provide his own fuel, prepare his own food, furnish his own shelter, make his own bed, and—perhaps most remarkable of all—transport himself by walking.

In these lessons are further the lessons of history—a stimulus to patriotism of the noblest order—for in the wilderness the land still lives as it was before the pioneers fashioned in and from it the civilization we know and enjoy.

With these lessons come also the understanding that physical, psychic, and spiritual human needs are such that wilderness recreation should always be available and, in fact, should be enjoyed to a much greater extent than it now is.

Thus recreational and educational values of the wilderness merge.

In a culture like that which we call modern we can be sure that it will be increasingly important for students, of the present and of future generations, to know what the wilderness has to teach—through their own experiences; through educators who are informed and corrected by wilderness experiences; through photographs, paintings, writings, and other educational and informational materials with a validity insured by a still living wilderness.

So long as wilderness exists in reality, providing actual resorts for human beings, giving a sense of actuality to pictorial and literary representations of the wilderness, and affording the scenes for further research, so long will the safeguards against an urban, industrial, mechanized ignorance of the facts of human life be effective.

There are monumental or historical values of the wilderness also, values which are closely related both to educational and recreational values. The wilderness I once described as "a piece of the long ago that we still have with us." It is highly prized by many people as such. It perpetuates on our continent not only the scene of the pioneering activities of the first white men in this hemisphere but also a still more ancient scene. The areas preserved are monuments to the pioneers' conquests, but they also are samples of the natural world without the influence of modern man. They have deep values in the continuing opportunity they afford to relive the lives of ancestors and thus, with also the anticipation of posterity's similar interest, to participate in the immortality of the generations.

The wilderness has profoundly important scientific values. These are similar to those of historical importance in depending on the preservation of areas as they existed, and exist, without the influence of modern man. These values too have an educational aspect, but their more precisely scientific importance is in relation to research. Their research uses are dual: They afford the scenes for fundamental investigations of the natural world of living creatures unmodified by man; they afford also "check" areas where none of the factors being compared in a particular study (land-use research, for example) have been operative.

The scientific values pertain not only to research and original investigation but also to the study and conservation that are essentially educational in their purpose. Wilderness areas, including the smaller natural areas and also the extensive wild regions, should accordingly be preserved for the sake of the field study that they make possible for students in each generation. They serve this purpose for the summer camps of youth organizations, for field stations of college summer-school classes, and also for the more advance excursions of graduate students.

And Aldo Leopold exclaimed: "As a matter of fact, there is no higher or more exciting sport than that of ecological observation."

So we have various needs for wilderness that are all derived form a need to maintain an awareness of our human relationships to all life, the need to guard ourselves against a false sense of our own sufficiency. We need to draw ourselves constantly toward the center of things and not allow our eccentricities to carry us off on a tangent, toward increasing unhappiness.

We are a part of the wildness of the universe. That is our nature. Our noblest, happiest character develops with the influence of wildness. Away from it we degenerate into the squalor of slums or the frustration of clinical couches. With the wilderness we are at home.

Some of us think we see this so clearly that for ourselves, for our children, our continuing posterity, and our fellow men we covet with a consuming intensity the fullness of the human development that keeps its contact with wildness. Out of the wilderness, we realize, has come the substance of our culture, and with a living wilderness— it is our faith—we shall have also a vibrant vital culture—an enduring civilization of healthful, happy people who, like Antaeus, perpetually renew themselves in contact with the earth.

This is not a disparagement of our civilization—no disparagement at all—but rather an admiration of it to the point of perpetuating it. We like the beef from the cattle grazed on the public domain. We relish the vegetables form the lands irrigated by virtue of the Bureau of Reclamation. WE carry in our packs aluminum manufactured with the help of hydroelectric power from great reservoirs. We motor happily on paved highways to the approaches of our wilderness. We journey in streamlined trains and in transcontinental airplanes to conferences on wilderness preservation. We nourish and refresh our minds from books manufactured out of the pulp of our forests. We enjoy the convenience and comfort of our way of living—urban, village, and rural. And we want this civilization to endure and to be enjoyed on and on by healthful, happy citizens.

It is this civilization, this culture, this way of living that will be sacrificed if our wilderness is lost. *What sacrifice!*

Conservation is both practical and idealistic, as is well demonstrated in our concern with wilderness preservation.

It is good and sound to realize that in preserving areas of wilderness we are recognizing our own true human interest. It seems good, ethical, to consider ourselves as members of a community of life that embraces the earth—and to see our own welfare as arising from the prosperity of the community.

Yet there may be danger in too conscious, too deliberate, too intent an effort to see all in terms of our own welfare. Jesus suggested that self-seeking is not the way to self-realization; not deliberately but through indirection human beings realize their best welfare, by losing sight of themselves.

It is a great satisfaction to be able to demonstrate to another that an unspoiled wilderness is important because it serves man's need for "escape," but going to the wilderness to escape from something is no certain way of actually being in the wilderness at all. The only way to escape from one's self in the wilderness is to lose one's self there. More realistically, the true wilderness experience is one, not of escaping, but of finding one's self by seeking the wilderness.

The sum of this moralizing may be in forsaking human arrogance and courting humility in a respect for the community and with regard for the environment.

The central human importance of such experience, I believe, constitutes profound evidence of need for wilderness areas.

An understanding of these fundamental needs, as well as the so-called more practical needs to meet recreational demands of people for wilderness experience—this understanding should inspire us anew to work for the perfection of a national program for wilderness preservation—a program to serve not only our own human needs but also those of the generations to follow.

This paper was delivered to the National Citizens Planning Conference on Parks and Open Spaces held in Washington, D.C., by the American Planning and Civic Association in 1955.

Alice and Howard Zahniser share a relaxing moment at Mateskared in the summer of 1960 with the faint image of Crane Mountain in the distance.

Where Wilderness Preservation Began

Howard Zahniser

Last summer, the summer of 1956, on the 9th of July, my wife and our four children and I left our home at the Nation's Capital and drove that day through the metropolis, New York City, and camped that night on the edge of a stretch of wilderness that extended for some 20 miles beyond the river along which we made our camp. Had we walked half way across that stretch of wilderness, we would have been at least ten miles from a road in any direction. In one day, at this late date in our American history, we had been able to travel from the capital of the country, through its metropolis, and camp that night on the edge of a vast expanse of wilderness. Such is the opportunity that we still have in this country.

That camp was on the Sacandaga River on the edge of the Forest Preserve.

To come up here again and be with you is certainly a great privilege. In a way, my coming is also an expression of the appreciation we all feel for what you people in New York State are doing for all of us when you maintain your Forest Preserve.

It is an important subject that we are now turning our thoughts toward—although I do not think it has been far from your thoughts during this convention—the subject, "Where Wilderness Preservation Began." We might change the subject just a little bit and say "Where Wilderness Preservation Begins," and we might say that, like charity, it begins right here at home. For this, in my way of feeling, is the place where the thing begins that I am so concerned about, and that is one of the reasons I am always so happy to come to the Adirondacks and the Catskills and Albany. It is a pleasure to be here, for I feel this is where wilderness preservation began, in a very real sense.

A century ago this year, in 1857, a writer by the name of S.H. Hammond wrote a book entitled *Wild Northern Scenes*. In this

69

volume he talked about his own Racquette River country. He began
to express fear lest civilization push its way to that wild country.
Here is what he said:

"Had I my way, I would mark out a circle of a hundred miles in
diameter and throw around it the protecting aegis of the Constitution.
I would make it a forest forever. The old woods should stand always
as God made them. . . and new woods should be permitted to supply
the place of the old so long as the earth remained."

That was written in 1857. The next year the *Atlantic Monthly* in
July carried an article by Henry David Thoreau about a series of trips
he made in 1853 in the Maine woods and, at the close of the article
in the July issue, Thoreau first presented a question as to why
shouldn't we have our national preserves, in which the bear and
panther, and some even of the hunter race, might still exist, and not
be civilized off the face of the earth—"not for idle sport or food, but
for inspiration and our own time recreation."

Some years earlier, in 1833, George Catlin, a Philadelphia lawyer
who became a great western artist and painter of western scenes,
writing a letter to the *Daily Commercial Advertiser* in New York City,
made a suggestion about having great national parks. He had suggested a government policy that would preserve some of these lands
"in their pristine beauty and wildness, in a magnificent park."

Those suggestions which we find in literature now had varying
degrees of attention at the time, I imagine. Frederick Law Olmsted
was enunciating similar principles when he was laying the plans for
Central Park in New York City. Others were speaking with great
appreciation of this wilderness that was being cherished here in the
Adirondacks.

J.T. Headley in his 1849 volume *The Adirondack; or Life in the
Woods* wrote: "I love nature and all things as God has made them. I
love the freedom of the wilderness"—a phrase that is of great interest
and is used a great deal by us. That was back in 1849. The book was
a compilation of letters that he had written to his friend, Henry J.
Raymond, a fellow reporter on the *New York Tribune*, who later
founded the *New York Times*, who himself later became a writer on

the Adirondacks. In 1855, he published a series of articles describing a Week in the Wilderness.

Most of us have heard about the Rev. William H.H. Murray, "Adirondack" Murray, whose 1869 book stirred so much interest and enthusiasm. One of the most interesting suggestions he made about the use of, and the appreciation of, the wilderness was a suggestion that churches send their pastors to the wilderness for vacation. He said when they came back—his words are too good to paraphrase: "For when the good dominie came back, swarth and tough as an Indian, elasticity in his step; fire in his eye; depth and clearness in his reinvigorated voice, wouldn't there be some preaching! And what texts he would have from which to talk to the little folks in the Sabbath school! How their bright eyes would open and enlarge as he narrated his adventures, and told them how the good Father feeds the fish that swim, and clothes the mink and beaver with their warm and sheeny fur. The preacher sees God in the original there, and often translates him better from his unwritten works than from his written word."

Of equal interest to me is a complaint the Reverend Mr. Murray made that, while he was writing these words, there was so much city noise in Boston, where he was writing, that it bothered him very much. To me, living in the midst of the clamor and roar of airplanes and the rush of traffic, I am interested to know that back in the midst of this earlier century, which I have considered quiet and serene, he was complaining: "How harshly the steel-shod hoofs smite against the flinty pavement beneath my window, and clash with rude interruptions upon my ear as I sit recalling the tranquil hours I have spent beneath the trees."

So noise, I guess, is a relative thing.

Those expressions of appreciation and those innovations from George Catlin in 1833, S.H. Hammond in 1857, and others are pleas for preserving areas of wilderness which must have fired the imagination and determination of Verplanck Colvin.

One of the reasons I like to come to Albany is that I remember that, a decade and a century ago—I think in 1847—Verplanck Colvin was born here in Albany. He walked the streets of this capital city and

worked in its halls and corridors for the preservation and appreciation of the Adirondacks, which he knew better than any other man
ever yet has known them. (I have read such tributes made by those
who should know better than I the degree of his acquaintance and
that of his possible rivals.) He took the measurement of these mountains. He was a surveyor, and, as William Chapman White said,
lectured without stopping for 20 years on the need for the creation of
an Adirondack Park or Timber Preserve. When the State Park
Commission was established in 1872, he became superintendent of
the state survey. "He was largely responsible for the creation of the
Adirondack Forest Preserve in 1885."

When the Legislature created a Forest Preserve and Commission
it said: "The lands now, or hereafter, constituting the Forest Preserve
shall be kept forever as wild forest lands." That was confirmed by
and strengthened by the 1894 Constitutional Convention, which
adopted Article 7, Section VII. (Later you took 7 and 7 to make Article
XIV.) [Zahniser then had the assembly stand and read in chorus,
from their printed programs, Article XIV, Section I: "The lands of the
state, now owned or hereafter acquired, constituting the forest preserve as now fixed by law, shall be forever kept as wild forest lands.
They shall not be leased, sold or exchanged, or be taken by any
corporation, public or private, nor shall the timber thereon be sold,
removed or destroyed."

That was an historic declaration of a sovereign state of the United
States declaring in its basic, fundamental law a purpose to keep forest
lands forever wild.

Among the "Selected Papers and Addresses" in the recently published volume entitled *Louis Marshall: Champion of Liberty* edited
by Charles Reznikoff, I have read with special interest the record of
the debate in the 1915 Constitutional convention on the Forest
Preserve. Mr. Marshall said then, in leading the debate in defense
of the Forest Preserve—he had been a member of the 1894 convention
also—"If I were asked to state what the most important action of the
convention of 1894 was, I should say without the slightest hesitation
that it was the adoption of *Section 7 of Article VII* of the Constitution
which preserved in their wild state the Adirondack and Catskill
forests."

This recognition of the value of wilderness as wilderness is something with which you have long been familiar here in New York State. It was here that it first began to be applied to the preservation of areas as wilderness.

The Federal government, by an Act of Congress approved by President Lincoln in 1864, granted the Yosemite Valley to the State of California upon the condition that it should be "held for public use, resort and recreation."

Two decades later, by an Act of Congress approved by President Grant, Yellowstone National Park was dedicated and set apart as a public park or pleasuring ground for the benefit and enjoyment of the people and provision made for the preservation from injury or spoliation of all timber, mineral deposits, natural curiosities, or wonders within said park, and their retention in their natural condition.

But here in New York, in 1885, by state legislative action and then in 1894 with Constitutional force, you, the people of New York State, used the term "forever wild" to describe a land management purpose. The people of this state thus began to cherish wilderness in a way that became more and more explicit as our great National Park System came to be valued more and more because it not only protected for the public its superlative areas of scenic wonders but also included areas of wilderness, and as the U.S. Forest Service began to establish primitive, wilderness, wild, and roadless areas within the National Forests.

It was in the southwest in 1924 that the type specimen of these National Forest areas was established by regional administrative action in the Gila National Forest. Aldo Leopold had begun in the 1920s to point out to the nation both the importance—recreational and ecological—of the national forest wildernesses and the growing threats to their persistence; and it was he who was chiefly responsible for the establishment of the Gila wilderness.

By the 1930s, when a national policy for wilderness preservation in the national forests had emerged, the great wilderness interpreter and champion from New York, Robert Marshall, had not only written his now classic interpretation entitled "The Problem of the Wilderness" but had also achieved his position on the staff of the U.S. Forest

Service where he was able to contribute so notably to the establishment of areas for preservation and to the formulation of regulations for their protection. He was a forester, a thinker, a writer, a
philanthropist. He had learned wilderness in the forever wild
Adirondacks. Here, with two companions, he had been the first to
climb all 46 of the peaks 4,000 feet high or higher. He had also seen
the great western areas of still living wilderness melting away "like
the last snowbank on some south-facing mountainside during a hot
afternoon in June." Activated by those observations and inspired by
his own knowledge, he set out to see preserved as many as possible
of the areas of wilderness throughout the U.S. under his jurisdiction.

Paul Schaefer has told me also how, on Mt. Marcy, he once saw Bob
Marshall stirred with the need for mobilizing people who would, as
citizens, support such governmental policies. It was Robert Marshall
from the Adirondacks who was the principal founder of The Wilderness Society. In our country, when any public purpose becomes
distinct, some organization is formed. We are experts in the forma-
tion of organizations. The Wilderness Society in the fullness of time
became the American people's public evidence of a distinctive purpose, and it was Robert Marshall from the Adirondacks who was
central in that organization.

Thus by the 1940s we had in fact in our National Park System, in
our National Forests, and in other Federal and State areas begun to
recognize the great wilderness preservation system. Through this
system of preserved areas, of which the Adirondack and Catskill
wildernesses are important units, we have proposed to maintain our
access to wildness, to what John Muir called "Fountains of Life."

Our great and expanding civilization is providing for the preservation of some areas that are still as the land was when we first saw it.
We realize that our civilization will eventually modify for human
exploitation every last area on the earth, except those that, through
human foresight and wisdom, have been deliberately set aside for
preservation. But we are persuaded that, through such a program of
designation, we can insure the existence of a system of wilderness
forever.

It is not too late. There are remnants of our primeval wilderness which we can, and must, still preserve—areas that we shall cherish more and more as our population pressures increase.

[Already] there has been developed here in New York State this unique concept. Here we do not need any new-fangled zoning. Here we already have one of the greatest pioneer zoning programs that has been developed in our great American experience of the management of public lands. The Forest Preserve itself is a zone, if you wish to call it that. The Adirondack and Catskill Parks are zones. This whole concept of the Forest Preserve within specially established state parks is New York's own zoning program. This is New York State's demonstration of an effective means for so managing lands as to serve specific public purposes, in this instance the preservation of wild forest lands forever wild.

The citizens of New York State, with their often demonstrated concern for the preservation of these wild forest lands should most assuredly, in my opinion and observation, look most searchingly at any zoning programs proposed as substitutes for their own wise provisions which so effectively began accomplishing zoning purposes long before ever the term became as popular as it now is. Surely, it is much better, in safeguarding the Forest Preserve, to be old-fashioned with parks and preserves that protect the wilderness, than to be brilliantly modern with something called zones that permit the destruction of the wilderness of these forest lands that is being cherished.

The citizen who lives in a Class A Residential Zone is no less distressed by the intrusion into his neighborhood of a commercial development simply because the intrusion was preceded by the zoning action of an up-to-date board of zoning adjustment. Similarly, the loss of New York State's wilderness will be no less shocking to its people simply because it may be accomplished by means of a zoning program.

I do not wish to go into great detail on that, but this is an aspect of the concept of the preservation of designated areas that seems full of meaning for the entire country and for all who are concerned with this problem.

I do, indeed, wish to emphasize the importance of establishing areas to be preserved. In such a program is our only hope. New York State, with such excellent experience in perpetuating wilderness in the Forest Preserve, can be of great help in seeing such a program firmly established nationally. That possibility now exists in some legislation we refer to as the Wilderness Bill, based on the same assumption in our national program that we have been discussing here: that our civilization is such that it is destined to occupy all areas except those we deliberately set aside for preservation unmodified; and, secondly, that if we are to have areas of wilderness existing in perpetuity, existing forever wild, we must have them through a public program for designating areas and protecting them faithfully through the years, as you have done here.

As we face this problem nationally, we do not have the opportunities that existed in 1885 and 1894. We come to the preservation of the wilderness—the raw material out of which we have fashioned our civilization—we come to the preservation of that basic resource last. The first and greatest of the resources is the last we have recognized as being in need of protection and, as we come to it, we find that the first of the assumptions to which I referred has already been realized in our national program. Every area of wilderness we have within our national public lands is now dedicated to some other purpose.

Fortunately, some of these purposes are absolutely consistent with the preservation of wilderness. The National Forests contain areas of wilderness that can persist while still serving their multiple purposes as National Forests for the preservation of watershed; for the use of sportsmen, and other recreationists; for research; and so forth. In many ways they can continue to serve their basic purposes as National Forest lands and still be preserved as wilderness. Similarly our national parks—48 of them, we calculate—have areas of wilderness. Out of 274 wildlife refuges, some 20 of them have areas of wilderness.

We therefore propose, as a national policy and a national program, to stabilize these areas as areas of wilderness within a National Wilderness System. We do not propose to change the administration of these areas. We do not propose to interfere with their integration with other areas of land handled by various agencies. We are suggesting merely at this opportune time in our history that we say to the administrators of these areas: "Treat them as wilderness." Wilderness is a character that land has while serving maybe another purpose that is consistent with it.

The central purpose in the Wilderness Bill that you may have heard a great deal about can thus be simply explained, and I appreciate this opportunity. I hope that you will think about it a bit and learn more about its provisions and apply the wisdom and experience you have gained here in New York State—apply the practical knowledge that you have—apply the political strength that you have—to spread from here throughout the nation the kind of program that you have worked out here through the years.

After all, it is not so important to know where wilderness began as it is to know that it is going on and on for generation after generation. You have a wonderful phrase here, "forever wild," which is an inspiration and a characterization of the nature of our own undertaking. We are not fighting a rear guard action. We are not simply trying to delay the inevitable taking over of all our wilderness lands by a fast moving civilization. We are trying—in this time of emergency, which is also a time of opportunity—to fashion a policy and develop a program that, if successful, will persist in perpetuity so that we shall always have these areas of wilderness. Let us not think that we are a minority fighting against a great majority which is inevitably going to crush us. We are not. We are representatives of a great majority.

Every time in my experience of a dozen years in working intimately in this field—every time that the people of the U.S. or of any State, have had an opportunity to express themselves on this issue, they have said, "Let's preserve our areas of wilderness."

If nationally we can do this, as I think we have done it here in New York State, through a policy which is enunciated and put firmly into our basic laws, and then can develop a practical, reasonable program within that policy, I think we can expect to have these areas of wilderness persist on and on. I know that it is a daring thing—a bold thing—for a man whose life lasts 40, 50, 60, 70, or 80 years to be talking in terms of eternity, but that is indeed what we are doing. We

78

are thinking of the eternity of the past that now exists in these areas of wilderness, and we have the presumption to say that we are going to do our best to make it possible for those areas from the eternity of the past to exist on into the eternity of the future. That is our faith.

This address was given to the New York State Conservation Council in annual convention in Albany, N.Y., October 4, 1957. The first Wilderness Bill had been introduced in Congress the previous year.

Zahnie traveled to all field hearings resulting in the Wilderness Act. On each trip he visited as many newspapers and radio and television stations as possible. This was the standard press portrait used from about 1959 on.

The Visionary Role
Of Howard Zahniser

Douglas W. Scott

The Wilderness Act—and the legislative struggle to enact it—involved the efforts and inspiration of countless people. A complete list would be impossible to draw up, but all involved would acknowledge the indispensible, visionary role of Howard Zahniser.

Zahniser was the true architect of the Wilderness Act, not merely because he drafted its language and catalyzed the endless details of the legislative campaign to see it enacted, but because he motivated so many to see the need, inspired thousands to think it possible, and emboldened all to persevere, even when discouragement set in. He was happiest, this remarkable leader, when his leadership was least visible, when a dozen others rose to voice the support he had engendered, speaking for wilderness from their own hearts.

"What made the difference," his closest ally, Dave Brower, wrote, "was one man's conscience, his tireless search for a way to put a national wilderness policy into law, his talking and writing and persuading, his living so that this Act might be born."

Zahniser, Brower, and their colleagues began from a fundamental premise: Wilderness is not merely for recreation and a "good time," but also for personal renewal as an essential need of all individuals and our entire culture.

"Out of the wilderness, we realize," Zahniser told the Sierra Club's 1951 Wilderness conference, "has come the substance of our culture, and with a living wilderness—it is our faith—we shall have also a vibrant culture, an enduring civilization of healthful citizens who renew themselves when they are in contact with the earth."

"Zahnie," as his friends called him, was a Pennsylvanian, educated at Greenville College in Illinois. In 1931 he joined the U.S. Biological Survey as an editor, later moving on to become head of the Information Division of the Bureau of Plant Industry. In 1945 he became executive secretary and editor of The Wilderness Society (of which he'd been a charter member in 1935). He began immediately to pursue a program to build support for wilderness—and to build the case for a wilderness law. As a result of his work, in 1948 the Legislative Reference Service of the Library of Congress issued a definitive study on the status of wilderness preservation, making a clear case that strengthened protection was essential. Zahniser saw to it that this report was widely distributed.

Zahniser first publicly outlined the idea of a wilderness law in 1951, at the Sierra Club's Wilderness Conference. How much wilderness can we afford to lose? he asked. No more, was his answer. "Our only hope to avert this loss is in our deliberate effort to preserve the wilderness that we have.

"It behooves us then to do two things," Zahniser went on. "First we must see that an adequate system of wilderness areas is designated for preservation, and then we must allow nothing to alter the wilderness character of the preserves. We have made an excellent start on such a program. Our obligation now—to those who have been our pioneers and to those of the future, as well as to our own generation—is to see that this program is not undone but perfected."

"At present," he observed, "there are so many test cases on our hands. . . that conservationists have not had the time or energy to pursue the all-important positive program that alone can prevent the constant recurrence of these controversies. Let's try to be done with a wilderness preservation program made up of a sequence of overlapping emergencies, threats, and defense campaigns! Let's make a concerted effort for a positive program that will establish an enduring system of areas where we can be at peace and not forever feel that the wilderness is a battleground."

Zahniser repeated the idea of the Wilderness Bill at the 1955 Sierra Club Wilderness Conference. In her summary, Club leader Charlotte Mauk wrote: "It was obvious that the individuals present were ready to say 'O.K.—we understand one another now and we have a pretty good idea of what we want. Let's go after it!'"

The fight to enact the Wilderness Bill was long and trying. Opponents used every legislative delaying tactic in the book. Zahniser was, in Dave Brower's tribute, "the constant advocate." Olaus Murie summed him up: "Eager to find an opportunity, taking advantage of every opening, always with good judgment in crises, and an unusual tenacity in lost causes."

After seven years of unquenchable advocacy, Zahniser died in his sleep on May 5, 1964, at age 58. Just two days earlier he had testified at the final hearings on the Wilderness Act.

Zahniser knew it would take unprecedented effort to build the National Wilderness Preservation System chartered by the Wilderness Act. But he had tremendous faith in those who would follow. "Through this measure," he said, "we have the great opportunity of establishing a policy and program that can be expected to endure, cherished and appreciated by those who will come after us, who will surely recognize that only because of the time and trouble that we are taking, in working out such a policy and program, will the wilderness have persisted to their day. With the enactment of this measure we shall cease to be in any sense a rearguard, delaying 'inevitable' destruction of all wilderness, but rather shall become a new vanguard with reasonable hopes that some areas of wilderness will be preserved in perpetuity."

At Mateskared, Alice Zahniser received a summons to the White House signing of the Wilderness Act in September 1964. She received a pen used in the signing by President Lyndon B. Johnson. Zahnie had died that May just days after testifying at the last public hearing on the legislation. Margaret E. "Mardy" Murie, to her right, represented herself and the late Olaus J. Murie, a former president of The Wilderness Society.

Afterword

Paul Schaefer

The circumstances surrounding my first meetings with Robert Marshall and Howard Zahniser, the two outstanding advocates of wilderness in this century, could hardly have been more opposite in the locations and the weather on the days I met them. It was about noon on a crystal clear July 15, 1932 when I first met Bob Marshall and his guide Herb Clark on the summit of mile-high Mount Marcy in the Adirondack Mountains. Fresh from about a year in the Arctic, Bob was renewing his acquaintance with these, his favorite mountains, before settling down behind a desk of the Forest Service of the U. S. Department of Agriculture in Washington, D.C.

Early in 1946, John Apperson and I had been requested to present our documentary photographs of the threatened South Branch of the Moose River to the North American Wildlife Conference in the Hotel Pennsylvania deep in the canyons of New York City. At stake was the imminent construction of Higley Mountain dam on that river. The day was overcast, bitterly cold, and it was snowing when we reached there. Immediately after our presentation Howard Zahniser came up to us and said he wanted to help us save that river.

"I am executive secretary of the Wilderness Society," he said. "I would like to see your Adirondack country."

Here was a man representing the organization that Bob Marshall had founded three years after our meeting on Mount Marcy. Then and there we agreed to meet in the mountains as soon as possible.

In August he and Ed Richard and I backpacked through Avalanche Pass in the High Peaks wilderness. Howard soon had a cabin not far from my log cabin near the Siamese Ponds wilderness. For him it was a place to rest from his intense activities in Washington. It was also a place to bring his family and make trips into the nearby wilderness and to mountain tops with me.

The major Adirondack problem at the time was our effort to block power dams on our rivers. We had put enough pressure on the state administration by 1947 that the governor called for abandonment of the Higley Mountain dam. But he proposed a larger Panther Mountain dam on the same river. This caused an uproar across the state. Finally, the speaker of the State Assembly decided that the legislature must find a way to get to the bottom of the rivers controversy. He created a Legislative Committee on River Regulation for New York State, and Assemblyman John Ostrander was named chairman of it. The committee scheduled public hearings across the state. Coincidentally, about this time we discovered that we had not only Panther Mountain dam to worry about, but a score more sprinkled throughout the Park, including Boreas Ponds, Hudson River, Chain Lakes, Piseco Lake, Salmon River, Thirteenth Lake, and Lake Lila.

The issue was simple and soon became clear to Zahniser. It was the question of the preservation of the river and lake lowlands of the Park as against their inundation. It was the preservation of the cradles of wildlife and deer yarding grounds, or the desolation of tens of thousands of acres of forests with cemeteries of tree stumps and mud flats.

The first public hearing by the Ostrander Committee was held in Schenectady on September 17, 1949. Zahniser was there along with 122 others from throughout the state and nation. From 1949 to 1951, the Ostrander Committee held eight public hearings. In some ways the hearing held in New York City on January 20 and 21, 1950 was the most important. The first day's overflow attendance included national as well as state organization representatives. The second day was devoted to officials of federal agencies, many of whom were friends of Zahniser. He had publicized the importance of this hearing in Washington and urged the officials to appear and give testimony. About 20 officials came, and together they made a strong case against Panther Mountain dam. The Fish and Wildlife Service, which had studied the Moose River region for several years with the U.S. Army Corps of Engineers presented a scholarly 25-point statement of the facts of wildlife in that region. They opposed the dam.

During the eight public hearings, conservationists, notably sportsmen, consistently had kept up the pressure of opposition. In 1951, organized labor, both A.F.L. and C.I.O., entered the conflict. There was considerable disagreement at first, but this changed in 1952, when Zahniser suggested to me that we needed to enlist Anthony Wayne Smith to our cause. Smith then represented both major labor organizations in Washington. His office took action immediately, and this labor influence on leaders of the legislature in New York State was a key element in our eventual success.

The Ostrander Committee finally won approval of the constitutional amendment that repealed the 1913 reservoirs amendment. The new amendment required the approval of the people in referendum for any future reservoir involving state land. Without this help by labor the long battle could not have been won.

During this period Zahniser gave numerous speeches to legislative study commissions, sportsmen, and other groups. He had begun serious work on his proposed National Wilderness Preservation Act. He observed more than once that the strong support for the protection of natural resources evidenced by statements made by more than 500 conservationists and service and women's clubs leaders at the Ostrander Committee hearings supported his authorship of that legislation.

Zahniser's actions on his National Wilderness Preservation Act took on new life after the Panther Mountain dam issue was over. In 1958 he gave a major speech on wilderness to the New York State Conservation Council. This was two years after the first Wilderness Bill was introduced in Congress, the first of 66 versions of that act that he wrote and rewrote.

Zahniser was active in the study a Joint Legislative Committee on Natural Resources for New York State was making in the designation of about one million acres of the Forest Preserve as wilderness and banning planes and motorized vehicles from those areas. This work in New York fitted perfectly his work on national wilderness legislation. Indeed, when Congressional public hearings were underway, the New York legislature, the New York State Conservation Council, the Association for the Protection of the Adirondacks, and other groups Howard had worked with testified in favor of the legislation.

On April 29, 1964, I received a letter from Howard in which he expressed the fact that he was exhausted from a final hearing before Congress, and he felt confident that it would become law. He also looked forward to returning to his Adirondack cabin in "lilac" time. Six days later the life of this magnificent man ebbed away. Four months later President Johnson signed the Wilderness Act.

Those legions of people who know the work that Howard Zahniser accomplished for the Adirondacks and for the American wilderness everywhere realize that his work was monumental and will be appreciated by posterity to an extent that those of us who witnessed his work cannot even imagine.